Empowering Researchers in Further Education

Empowering Researchers in Further Education

Yvonne Hillier and Jill Jameson

with a preface and introductory chapter
by Andrew Morris

Trentham Books
Stoke on Trent, UK and Sterling, USA

Trentham Books Limited

Westview House	22883 Quicksilver Drive
734 London Road	Sterling
Oakhill	VA 20166-2012
Stoke on Trent	USA
Staffordshire	
England ST4 5NP	

First published 2003

British Library Cataloguing-in-Publication Data
A catalogue record for this book is available from the British Library

ISBN 1 85856 285 6

Cover photograph:
NASA image – '*Cygnus Loop Supernova Blast Wave*'
NASA Centre: Hubble Space Telescope Centre
Image #: PR93-01 Date : 01/01/1993

Designed and typeset by Trentham Print Design Ltd., Chester and printed in Great Britain by Cromwell Press Ltd., Wiltshire.

Contents

List of figures and tables • vi

Acknowledgements • viii

Preface • xiii

Introduction • xvii

Section One – Getting involved

Chapter 1
The case for research • 3

Chapter 2
Changing policy issues facing the sector • 15

Chapter 3
Framing questions of research:
developing professional knowledge • 35

Section Two – Finding out the main issues

Chapter 4
Small-scale research: action research and
reflective practice • 51

Chapter 5
Practical considerations in designing and
conducting research • 59

Chapter 6
Finding information and literature reviews • 71

Chapter 7
Ethical considerations • 83

Section Three – Collecting data – some key methods

Chapter 8
Interviews and Focus Groups • 101

Chapter 9
Questionnaires and surveys • 125

Chapter 10
Working with statistics • 143

Section Four – Making use of research and going further

Chapter 11
Making use of research • 165

Chapter 12
Going further: joining a community of research practice • 175

References • 187

Index • 191

List of figures and tables

Figure 2.1 A typology of FE institutional and practitioner
responses to policy documents • 30

Figure 3.1 Framing questions of knowledge • 42

Figure 3.2 Spidergram of themes • 43

Figure 3.3 Venn diagram showing
three overlapping issues • 45

Figure 3.4 Issues for consideration regarding
disaffected 14-16 year olds • 45

Figure 5.1 Decision matrix • 63

Figure 5.2 Fields of study • 69

Figure 6.1 Web search example • 80

Figure 7.1 consent form • 88

Figure 8.1 Structured interview • 103

Figure 8.2 Semi-structured interview • 104

Figure 8.3 Unstructured interview • 105

Figure 8.4 Example of a focus group process • 115

Figure 9.1 Example questionnaire • 128

Figure 9.2 Example learner support questionnaire – closed questions • 140

Figure 9.3 Example learner support questionnaire – open questions • 140

Figure 10.1 Pie chart of scores on physics test • 146

Figure 10.2 Bar chart of scores of physics test • 147

Figure 10.3 Example of a normal distribution • 149

Figure 10.4 standard deviation • 151

Figure 10.5 Correlation of tutorials and grades • 156

Figure 11.1 Strategy for implementing FE practitioner research findings linked to policy • 171

Figure 11.2 Contents • 172

Figure 11.3 Suggested draft of subsections within chapters against contents list for report • 173

Table 10.1 Achievement rates for Certificate and NVQ awards • 158

Table 10.2 Chi Square Calculation for Achievement Rates • 159

Acknowledgements

We would like to thank Dr Andrew Morris, in particular, for his significant and invaluable contribution to this book in the Preface and Introductory chapter, and for being a wise and funny third member of the team! We thank our colleagues Dr Joe Harkin, Ros Clow, Graham Knight and the Learning and Skills Development Agency for the use of the questionnaire from the research study, *Recollected in tranquility? FE teachers' perceptions of their initial teacher training* (LSDA, 2003). We thank Professor Mary Hamilton for permission to use the consent form from the Changing Faces Project, funded by ESRC. We thank our partners and families for their endless good-humoured patience in supporting the writing of this work. At the University of Greenwich, we acknowledge with thanks Patrick Ainley for his helpful comments in relation to learning and skills policy, and Clare Cummings for her endless support and help with administration in the early stages of this work. At City University we thank Jon Blanchard for his enthusiastic support for tracking down references.

Dedication

Yvonne Hillier: to John
Jill Jameson: to Peter, Phyllis, Kevin and Imogen

Note on the authors

Dr Yvonne Hillier is Acting Head of Department of Continuing Education at City University. She has over 20 years' experience of working in adult, further and higher education.

Dr Jill Jameson is Director of Lifelong Learning at the University of Greenwich, a senior manager in lifelong learning, continuing education and partnership, with over 14 yrs F/HE senior management experience.

Dr Andrew Morris is the Programme Director, National Educational Research Forum and Research Manager, Learning and Skills Development Agency. Andrew initiated the national Learning and Skills Research Network.

All are members of the National Planning Group for the Learning and Skills Research Network and the Learning and Skills Network London and South East, linked with the Learning and Skills Development Agency.

Glossary

ALI	Adult Learning Inspectorate
AOC	Association for Colleges
BERA	British Educational Research Association
BIDS	Bath information and database service
BSA	Basic Skills Agency
DES	Department of Education and Science
DfEE	Department for Education and Employment
DfES	Department for Education and Skills
DoE	Department of Employment
ESRC	Economic and Social Research Council
ET	Employment training
EU	European Union
FE	Further Education
FEDA	Further Education Development Agency
FEFC	Further Education Funding Council
FENTO	Further Education National Training Organisation
FERN	Further Education Research Network
FEU	Further Education Unit
GNVQ	General National Vocational Qualification
HE	Higher Education
HEFCE	Higher Education Funding Council for England
HNC	Higher National Certificate
HND	Higher National Diploma
ICT	information and communications technology
ILT	information and learning technology
LEA	Local Education Authority

LLL	Lifelong Learning
LSC	Learning and Skills Council
LLSC	Local Learning and Skills Council
LSDA	Learning and Skills Development Agency
LSRN	Learning and Skills Research Network
LSRC	Learning and Skills Research Centre
MIS	Management information system
NCVQ	National Council for Vocational Qualifications
ND	National diploma
NFER	National Foundation for Educational Research
NIACE	National Institute for Adult and Continuing Education
NTO	National Training Organisation
NVQ	National Vocational Qualification
OECD	Organisation for Economic Co-operation and Development
OPAC	Open Public Access Catalogue
OU	Open University
PGCE	Postgraduate Certificate in Education
QAA	Quality Assurance Agency
QCA	Qualifications and Curriculum Authority
RAE	Research Assessment Exercise
RDA	Regional Development Agency
TEC	Training and Enterprise Council
TVEI	Technical and Vocational Education Initiative
UfI	University for Industry
UK	United Kingdom
WEA	Workers Education Association

Preface

Andrew Morris

A book about research, specifically for practitioners in post-16 education and training, is much to be welcomed. This book, with its practical approach grounded in clearly articulated theory, has been designed for use by teachers, trainers, lecturers and the galaxy of guidance, library, technical, marketing and learning support staff who make up the practitioner world. Research activity has been growing within the learning and skills sector in recent years: on participation, teaching and learning, finance, leadership, skills and economic development, for example. It is attracting greater attention from universities and government departments, as well as from education and training providers themselves. Yet this renewed emphasis on research still barely impinges on the daily life of busy practitioners. Indeed, throughout the twenty-five years of my own teaching career, the gap between the teacher in the classroom and the evidence accumulating in academe appears to have stubbornly remained.

When I entered teaching at the age of twenty seven I felt I had found a truly satisfying vocation. Like many Further Education (FE) Teachers, I had worked initially outside education and had come to it with a sense of purpose and hope. I found the human challenges profound, trying to understand the approaches of different people to learning (usually quite unlike my own) and figuring out how to communicate complex concepts in manageable ways. Compared with other types of work, the opportunity to teach seemed exhilarating and the responsibility for influencing people's lives truly awe-inspiring! Further education clearly provided high quality learning experiences for countless students, many of whom felt disappointment with their earlier ones. Their purposes were utterly varied: working telecommunications apprentices, needing to qualify; business administration students hell bent on jobs, 'A' level and Access students set on university; and teaching approaches needed to vary accordingly.

As a consequence of this variety, teachers were able to test out and adapt different ways of teaching for different purposes. My own timetable brought me in touch equally with academically orientated learners whose occupational goals lay far ahead, trainees for whom getting a job was an immediate goal, and mature students for many of whom the workplace had already proved frustrating. For each a different regime was demanded, whether for assessing student work, discussing issues, or learning through discovery. In short, the circumstances for teaching were rich and complex and so were the opportunities for experimentation. I recall this experience not merely as reminiscence, but for a more critical purpose – to reflect on the kind of evidence, including the trials and errors of my own making, that played a part in my own professional development.

Trial and error

As most teachers do, I listened carefully to students, encouraged them to question my utterances and to express the difficulties they experienced in trying to understand things. I tried out various classroom dynamics, student presentations, peer learning, small group project work, for example, and informally noted their effects on achievement and motivation. I discussed approaches with other teachers and tried to distinguish those deriving from their personalities from others linked to the subject or the types of learner they taught.

In retrospect, it seems remarkable how little reference I ever made, as a developing professional, either to a 'science' (or knowledge) base or to a 'technology' (or procedural) base to guide my experimentation. My biggest surprise on entering teaching was not in fact the problems presented by the students, nor indeed the demands of teaching itself, but the extraordinary level of responsibility given to me on the basis of such little know-how. As one of the great professions, contributing as much to the overall well being of society and the economy as medicine or architecture, I had assumed teaching would be based on well-attested knowledge derived from careful research. Instead, I experienced it as a kind of artistry, relying on skilful and essentially intuitive use of technique; knowing, for example, just when to switch from whole-class to small-group teaching, from general theory to particular cases, from verbal reasoning to practical demonstration. But even then, and more so now, I sensed that part at least of this art should be informed by more extensive research than my personal reflections on experience.

If my practice as a teacher had shown little regard for evidence, my life in management involved none at all. Survival seemed to be the key issue in management, and this called for a quick-fix approach to problems and a tolerance for vagueness about professional procedure. Neither seemed appropriate for the complex organisational and cognitive challenges that college managers actually faced. In building tower blocks or performing heart surgery, professional expertise rests on research evidence. Educating tomorrow's citizens, no less a task, calls for much the same.

The need for change

My own experience of managing in colleges suggested that, despite heroic efforts by individual team leaders, coordinators, departmental heads and strategic teams, basic problems of delivery persisted, year in, year out. Achievements seemed to differ significantly and consistently between similar groups of students taught by different teachers; some departments or institutions appeared unable to overcome recurrent problems that others did. National curricular and assessment initiatives often seemed badly framed, sometimes even damaging to effective provision; money intended to improve learner experience achieved this only on occasion. I gradually came to appreciate that these manifestations arose from a more fundamental and pervasive problem affecting government, the profession and its institutions, the absence of a clearly articulated base of research evidence and theory upon which professionals could draw for their practical and policy-making work.

Development and research

This brief sketch of personal experience outlines the case for research and development applied to educational practice. The purpose of both is to help improve practice. Development is commonplace in Further Education as institutions cope with new qualifications, assessment strategies, learning materials and teaching approaches, often introduced with extraordinary rapidity. Research is needed that interacts with such development. It deepens understanding of issues by adopting a systematic approach to gathering and analysing information or concepts. Its value lies less in its ability to fix immediate problems, and more in its capacity to illuminate persistent ones. To serve this role, the rigour of its methods is critical: they must enable analysis to be generalised beyond its immediate context.

Extending the skills, knowledge and understanding of the practitioner, to help them to contribute to this task, is the purpose of this book. It is designed to encourage the teacher, guidance worker, librarian, marketing officer, technician or manager to engage in appropriate ways with research. It may inspire some to join in with the planning of new projects, others to analyse existing findings or help interpret them for practical use. Some may wish to go further and undertake action-research themselves, or to embark on further research-orientated study. Whichever path interests you, I am confident you will find this book useful and hope that it inspires you to join with some of the countless others who share your desire.

May 2003

Introduction

What do we think about when we use the word 'research'? For many people, it conjures up images of laboratories and people wearing white coats and goggles. For others, it may mean people sitting in a library, speaking in hushed tones, and writing studiously. It could mean people with clipboards walking around the streets asking passersby to take part in a short interview. These images of research are powerful influences on the way we expect to hear about and use research.

Where does research take place? Many readers will know that there are research institutions and organisations which have the sole purpose to conduct research into certain areas, for example the National Federation for Educational Research (NFER). Most people in the United Kingdom (UK) will have been reading about the way research is funded in universities, and how current government thinking intends to concentrate funding for research in an elite group of universities.

This book aims to break the mould of everyday notions of research when applied to one educational sector, the Learning and Skills Sector (LSC), and in particular, Further Education (FE). Andrew Morris wryly notes in his preface that much of the everyday practice in the FE sector makes little reference to research, and yet, despite this, people who work in the sector have much responsibility for practical decision-making and delivery that would benefit from research. We realised many years ago that it was time to acknowledge the research that already *does* take place in the sector, and to foster the *capability* to undertake research amongst practitioners.

So what do we mean by research?

Drawing upon the Oxford English Dictionary definition of research as 'the careful search or inquiry' and 'course of critical investigation', we believe that research is a *process* of collecting information. The word 'research' stems from the French *rechercher*, meaning to seek or search again. 'Seeking' is a delightful word. It implies action, and intention. 'Searching again' implies ongoing action and commitment. If we consult a thesaurus, research is linked to a number of words including analysis, delving, examination, scrutiny, exploring and probing. There is something about research that involves action, intent and commitment to finding out something.

Where research?

Where does research take place? Research already takes place in the Learning and Skills Sector and has great potential to expand. This sector is vast. Research in the LSC sector might cover virtually every formal programme of learning that can be undertaken by people aged 14 and above who are no longer at school, or even within further education.

Communities of practice

People who work in the Learning and Skills Sector belong to subgroups. They may belong to subject discipline networks, and will certainly be placed in management groups, often in schools or faculties in larger colleges, and in training departments in larger workplace training organisations. They may be part of regional and national groups, for example if they verify programmes for awarding bodies. All of these groupings are *communities of practice* (Lave and Wenger, 1991). In other words, their professional practice is not something they undertake in isolation. FE consists of a major community of practice, within which are many smaller communities.

We believe that research within the FE sector provides opportunities to work within these *existing* communities of practice. We also believe that people who wish to undertake research can create new 'communities of practice'. A central theme of this book is that research can be done collaboratively, both within organisations and within networks that operate across organisations and institutions.

A recent LSC survey into learner satisfaction (LSC, 2002) showed that learners in adult and community learning provision were overwhelmingly satisfied with their programmes of learning. This information not only provides a spur to continue such good work. It also reinforces the notion that there is a community of practice in adult and community learning that clearly has already developed approaches to teaching and learning, amongst other things, that ensure that people are learning successfully.

Who researches?

As we have noted elsewhere (Jameson and Hillier, 2003) much existing research about further education has been conducted by people who work in higher education. This research has been conducted *on* FE, rather than *in* FE, *by* FE practitioners. We are aware that there is enormous capacity to conduct research within the FE sector, not only because numerous people already undertake small-scale research as part of higher degrees and professional qualifications, but also because they take part in funded research projects or commissioned work.

Within the Further Education National Training Organisation Standards (FENTO 1999), the developments for initial qualifications for teachers of basic skills (FENTO 2002), management standards (FENTO 2001) and the leadership qualification for FE principals, there is a now a requirement for continuing professional development (CPD) that demands reflection on, and developments in, professional practice. This kind of advanced professional practice is, in effect, 'research' by another name, linked directly into the workplace.

What kind of research?

In our book, we have tried to draw on a variety of contexts in which research can take place. Within the numerous communities of practice in FE, there are a number of domains, including: teaching and learning, market research, pastoral care, learning support, administration, student services, management of resources, management of staff, knowledge management, and the use of technology. Each of these activities has a research literature to support its practice. We will not be focusing on each of these areas in great detail, but will concentrate primarily on general issues relating to educational research. There is a vast literature on educational research and each chapter will suggest further reading. However, it is important to highlight the controversies that surround educational research. We therefore need to 'set out our stall' regarding our own understanding of educational research.

Hammersley (2003) reminds us of the range of meanings, implicit and explicit, when we talk about educational research. Do we expect educational research to have educational outcomes? Do we want our research to be effective, regardless of the context in which this takes place? He summarises many of the controversies in educational research. There are debates about how practice and theory can be distinguished or synthesised. There are also debates about ontology: about how we create meaning for concepts as they are developed. There are many areas of human activity: research is primarily an inquiry into these. To research these, we need to consider our under-lying ways of thinking and knowing. Habermas (1987) talks about three kinds of inquiry: *technical, practical* and *emancipatory.* Technical inquiry seeks control over our environment. Practical inquiry asks 'what works'. Emancipatory inquiry seeks to increase human autonomy. Habermas argues that all three approaches are necessary to help us conduct our inquiry about the world. We have tried in the following chapters to address all three forms of inquiry.

Empowering researchers

We believe that research can be an empowering process. By taking time to reflect on a particular issue, to devise a question for inves-tigation, and to find a means to try to answer that question is very liberating. It gives power to the investigator over the everyday prac-tices s/he engages in. By working with colleagues, a practitioner can engage in advancing the community of practice, and in developing personal and shared understandings of what it is that people do.

We also believe that having the knowledge and skills to undertake research enables people to challenge but also to work effectively with initiatives and practices that are increasingly required of them. Such knowledge and skill can therefore improve the practices within the sector but also make a difference to the people at the centre of the sector's work: the learners.

To be partners in research endeavours, practitioners need knowledge and understanding of the research process: its underlying theories and debates, as well as its limitations. We believe that such knowledge and understanding is indeed empowering. Linked with a commitment to continual questioning and critically reflecting on practice, it provides the cornerstone for the dynamic practice that is required in further education today.

Structure of this book

In the preface, Andrew Morris traces his experience as a teacher and manager in further education who discovered with surprise the general lack of evidence-based practice in education. Andrew is amongst those, including the Department for Education and Skills (DfES), the Learning and Skills Development Agency (LSDA), and the Centre for Evidence-informed Education Policy and Practice Information (EPPI centre) at the London University Institute of Education, who are calling for a change in educational practice to reflect greater recognition of the ways in which practitioners can benefit from undertaking evidence-based research.

Our call for research to inform practice is followed up throughout the four main sections of this book:

• Section one: Getting involved

• Section two: Finding out the main issues

• Section three: Data collection methods

• Section four: Making use of research and going further

Section one: getting involved

Andrew Morris introduces the background case for practitioner research in more detail in chapter 1, relating the history by which the Further Education Development Agency (FEDA) set up a new network for research in FE, the Further Education Research Network (FERN), following a seminal conference in 1997. In chapter 2, we look at the policy issues facing the sector, and the way in which evidence-based research is best used to shape these. In chapter 3, we examine how to frame questions of research in the development of practitioners' professional knowledge, examining the different kinds of knowledge available to us, with practical examples from further education.

Section two: finding out the main issues

This section gives an overview of the main issues affecting practitioners carrying out small-scale research projects. In chapter 4, we examine the field of small-scale research in general, and consider the overall benefit of carrying out action research and reflective practice to inform our development. Chapter 5 provides an overview of planning for small-scale research projects, through the practical example of a case study in designing a research project. In chapter 6, we consider how to find information for practitioner research projects, looking in some detail at web-based sources and the ways in which practitioners can carry out literature reviews when proposing, developing and writing up research reports. In chapter 7, we consider the detailed and problematic question of ethics for research.

Section three: data collection methods

This section provides a practical toolkit of data collection methods for small-scale researchers in FE. Methods for holding interviews and focus groups are examined in chapter 8, while in chapter 9 we provide an overview of the methodology for questionnaires and surveys. In chapter 10, we provide a straightforward guide for making sense of the complex field of statistics that we hope will be useful for practitioners having difficulties with this area.

Section four: making use of research and going further

This section concludes with an overview of making use of research and the way in which practitioners can go further in their research activities. In chapter 11 we suggest ways in which practitioners can make profitable use of their research to improve and develop their practice. In chapter 12, we offer suggestions for taking practitioner research further by participating, for example, in communities of professional practice.

References and Index

We include at the end of each chapter some key references relating to the chapter to enable practitioners to 'find out more' about that particular topic.

Section One
Getting Started

Chapter 1
The case for research

Andrew Morris

Involvement in research can play an important part in our professional development as individuals – it helps illuminate our practices.
It has played an important role in educational change over many
years. In the 1960s and 70s, schoolteachers developed curricula and
teaching practices through action-research, often in association with
university-based researchers.

In the following decade, the technical and vocational initiative
(TVEI) engaged teachers in curricular and pedagogic developments
in schools and colleges. The growth of Training and Enterprise Councils (TECs) encouraged development projects, particularly related to
the implementation of National Vocational Qualifications (NVQs)
and General National Vocational Qualifications (GNVQs), and to the
labour market in general. The setting up of the Further Education
Funding Council (FEFC) in the early 1990s led to further development projects that encouraged colleges to develop their competitive-
ness and responsiveness to employers and local communities.

Some colleges also developed research links with Higher Education
Institutions (HEIs), not least in relation to credit accumulation and
transfer. Teacher-based research is not limited to the UK. It
flourishes for example in the United States, in which community
college research journals report regularly on practitioner research on
pedagogic issues, social issues such as achievement by minority
groups and business issues such as staff careers and college

finances. Across the European Union (EU), research, sometimes involving practitioners, is the focus of CEDEFOP, the EU centre for research into vocation education and training. Its website 'training village' is used by teacher-researchers throughout the EU.

The case for research in further education extends, however, beyond activity at an individual level. Research-based evidence is needed for decision-making at all levels. Teaching teams need to understand their client groups, and how to recruit and motivate them. Institutions need to understand how their curriculum offer matches needs in their communities, such as the demand for workplace skills, for community development, and for progression from school. Local Learning and Skills Councils (LLSCs), Local Education Authorities (LEAs) and Regional Development Agencies (RDAs) need evidence of trends to inform their strategic planning. National government, with its many agencies for inspection, funding and development, needs to draw on research-based evidence for developing and implementing policy.

The Further Education Development Agency (FEDA)
The case for more and different research in further education was understood at the time the Further Education Development Agency was created in 1995. This unique organisation was formed by merging a curriculum development body, the Further Education Unit (FEU), with a professional development centre, the FE Staff College. FEDA had a division devoted to research and development and was given a remit to develop 'strategic' research on post-16 education and training. It devoted funds to advancing both research and development activity and to start to define what strategic, or longer term, more fundamental research would look like in further education. This led, for example, to studies of learners' perspectives on progressing from school to college, community perspectives on the role of an FE college and business perspectives on the FE role in local economic development.

In parallel with this strategic drive for more effective research *on* the sector, a bottom-up movement began to develop for research *in* the sector. A survey of research activity in colleges undertaken by Martin Johnson of the FEU in 1997 (Johnson 1997) demonstrated that a certain amount of research was in fact already taking place in colleges. At the same time, a highly significant workshop was organised by Peter Davies at the former Staff College entitled *Research in Further Education*. This led to a group of enthusiasts meeting together and deciding to form a Further Education Research Network (FERN), which was to be supported by FEDA.

The FE Research Network (FERN)

The planning group of the embryonic FERN network drew up a statement of purpose and values and invited people to become part of it. The aim was to raise the profile of FE research and to build a community around it. The approach would be to bring together the FE and HE sectors so that their contributions would reinforce rather than rival one another. Growth of the network was to depend on establishing regionally-based groups and to help people develop their skills, knowledge and understanding together. Volunteers came forward from both FE and HE to set up the new network.

This bottom-up initiative led in December 1997 to the first of what was to be a regular series of annual conferences at which a wide range of workshops and papers were organised, demonstrating the diversity of FE research activity in both sectors and the significant numbers of people who wanted to see it enhanced. The network and its conference, renamed *Learning and Skills* in 2000, to incorporate work-based and adult and community-based learning, have since gone from strength to strength. Conferences are now regularly addressed by government ministers, leading academics and policy officials, and attendances have increased steadily each year.

Learning and Skills Research Journal

In parallel with this growing network of practitioners, a journal was developed at FEDA, with the express purpose of addressing teachers and managers in colleges as well as researchers and policy officials. Called *College Research*, it aimed to communicate the findings of research in and on FE for teachers, managers and policy officials as well as for researchers themselves. Articles were to be short, capable of being read in a few minutes, and were to highlight messages for the practitioner. The journal, renamed *Learning and Skills Research* in 2000, has demonstrated the richness of research in and about the sector and has shown how it can be reported in a way that bridges the gap between researcher and practitioner.

R&D Toolkit

The rapidly emerging FE research community needed more than effective communications. It also needed professional development. The network adopted a collaborative approach to enhancing its skills, knowledge and understanding. An *R&D Toolkit* was devised, providing structured learning materials for mixed groups of researchers and practitioners to use in sessions organised up and down the country. In these, people with differing levels of previous knowledge shared their perspectives and learned about new concepts together.

At the time of writing, the range of topics in the *R&D Toolkit* is constantly growing but covers fundamental issues such as *distinguishing research from development*, technical issues such as *questionnaire design* and practical ones, such as *project management*. Participants are able to fit sessions into their crowded timetables and benefit from making contact with others as well as from deepening their understanding. For some, it acts as a starting point for further study at masters or doctoral level.

Underlying issues

This brief historical sketch serves to show that a culture of research has begun to develop across the post-16 sector in recent years. This process has not only led to more activity but has also catapulted FE researchers into parallel developments affecting educational research as a whole. Some of these are addressed in the remainder of this chapter.

Collaboration

In endeavouring to link research in the FE and the HE communities, differences in purpose become apparent. FE institutions often need research to shed light on issues of direct practical concern. Marketing teams, for example, need to research the profile of people not enrolling at college to influence strategies for reaching them. Strategic planners need to understand trends in the labour market and the demand for skills in order to make longer term plans for courses and departments. Teachers need to reflect systematically on their pedagogic experience to inform new teaching strategies. For these marketeers, teachers and managers, research activity does not form a major or even a required part of their primary role.

In universities on the other hand, research is usually a requirement of academic staff and for many, forms a significant part of their working lives. Publication of research papers in journals refereed by their peers is one of the key ways in which university academics gain professional recognition and the resources that flow from it. For research in this academic tradition working on the leading edge, creating new knowledge and adding to theory, are valued highly. The 'knowledge transfer' role of universities aims to spread and link this knowledge into regional communities.

When HE-based and FE-based researchers come together, the clash of fundamental purposes can easily lead to difficulties. Academics may appear less interested in the problems of daily practice or the implementation of new policy, while FE practitioners may appear too dismissive of theory or the depth of argument in the research literature. The Research Network recognised this problem and addressed it by organising discussions at regional meetings in which the various parties described their activities to one another. A structure was created which enabled people to learn to give value to each other's forms of knowledge and experience. After this preliminary stage, a scheme of regionally-based projects was set up to be planned and undertaken collaboratively. These projects have directly confronted the difficulties of communicating, agreeing purposes and methods across the sectors. The series of research reports from these projects, published by LSDA, illustrates how the difficulties of collaboration were overcome (Taylor, 2002, Davies, 2001)

One approach to managing collaborative research is to conceptualise the process of research, including its planning, execution and aftermath, as a series of interdependent stages (Morris, 2002). The 'planning' stages involve identifying the priority issues for a project, the research questions and the active partners. These then lead to a specification stage in which aims, objectives, methods and outputs are planned together. The 'investigative' stages, perhaps involving literature studies, data gathering and analysis, then lead on to an 'influencing' phase. Different members of a collaborative team, for example college staff, HE researchers and local policy-based staff, are then called upon to contribute their specific skills and knowledge at appropriate stages. Some are more involved in planning, some in the analysis and others in taking forward the outcomes into practical situations. What appear initially as potential areas for conflict become starting points for delineation of role.

Regionality

Although regions do differ significantly in their economic profile, it is for other reasons that the regional networks have proved so important for research. They have enabled people to come together, to address the difficulties of collaborative working and to develop a set of working relationships to overcome them. These important relationships have not been submerged in a context of national policy or of national players. Flexibility at regional level has also allowed topics to be identified that people judge to be priorities for them. The sense of ownership then leads on to greater engagement and interest in the outcomes. One of the significant lessons for individuals reading this book, is to consider the value to be gained from joining with others in undertaking any research venture. Apart from the social benefit of working with others, it enables different perspectives, a wider range of methods and of critical feedback to influence your work.

Forms of knowledge

Another of the deeper issues that emerged during the growth in the research network was the variety of forms of knowledge relevant to educational research. Knowledge valued for academic purposes is codified explicitly in the requirements for publication in journals and for achieving funding through the Higher Education Funding Council for England (HEFCE) Research Assessment Exercise (RAE) and through the research councils such as the Economic and Social Research Council (ESRC). These lay stress on the originality of the work, its potential to add to the body of knowledge in academic disciplines and its relative validity or authenticity. FE teachers, on the other hand, may well be less concerned with whether a piece of research is original than with whether it is useful to them; for FE managers even more so, and the extent to which it informs the objectives to which they are working.

LSDA and the Research Network have approached these issues by developing practical means for expressing the value of different forms of knowledge. Knowledge gained through extensive practical experience is identified through practical workshops, practitioner surveys and case studies. Conferences are multi-stranded, allowing developers to communicate through workshops, researchers through papers and policy people through round-table discussion. The *Learning and Skills Research* journal is also multi-stranded, with separate sections for policy commentaries, research papers and reports of innovative development.

In a good illustration of the adage 'nothing is more practical than a good theory', Charles Desforges described in a speech to a Research Network conference, the concept of 'knowledge transformation' (Desforges, 2001). He points out that in many spheres, knowledge comes to the attention of practitioners before it is taken up by researchers – 'practice leads theory'. In addition, knowledge frequently needs to be transformed before it can be usefully applied to improving practice. This process of transformation inevitably requires the skills and understanding of practitioners to be brought into conjunction with those of the researcher. In realising this process, LSDA programmes, such as the Raising Quality and Achievement (RQA) or the Quality in Information and Learning Technology (QUILT) programmes were designed in the light of research evidence and the developmental needs of practitioners. These programmes in turn funded workshops, networks and publications in which theoretical, empirical and practical forms of knowledge were mixed together, discussed and acted upon.

In a similar spirit, projects designed by regional research networks draw on differing forms of knowledge and engage researchers and practitioners in transforming them. The Yorkshire and Humberside project in 2002, for example, involved teachers recording in diaries their live experiences of college inspection, a university professor in developing and advising on the method, regional LSDA staff in managing the partnership and project. At the same time, ways of creating greater influence through research have been developed nationally by LSDA. New publication formats including brief summaries of findings are publicly available through the internet and are distributed to providers and policy bodies at all levels, nationally, regionally and locally.

Putting research to use

Both practitioners and decision-makers need to use the findings of research to help them with the practical issues they face in class-rooms, workshops and committee rooms. From their points of view, the problems are how to find, understand, judge and apply evidence that will help them. They need access to what is known reliably about teaching styles, assessment methods, recruitment and induction processes and to see how it could be applied to groups of learners, curriculum areas and local settings that are meaningful to them. For some, there is a thirst to reach out beyond the familiar anecdotes, personal opinions, and traditions that prevail in working life. What is commonplace is for such people to have little time available, to have difficulty in choosing key pieces to read and to find written material remote, unintelligible and too general for the specific setting in which they work.

Conversely, university-based researchers tend to focus more on contributing to knowledge and theory in academic disciplines than on applying this to problems in public services, like education, largely because they are rewarded for doing so. Applied research in education is relatively underdeveloped in the UK. The reasons for this are critically analysed in a report by the prestigious international body, the Organisation for Economic Coordination and Development (OECD, 2002). It suggests a number of ways forward, from changing the funding allocation mechanism (the Research Assessment Exercise) to enhancing the National Education Research Forum (http://www.nerf.gov.uk).

Strategies for making an impact

In recent years, parts of the research community have begun to address ways in which its work could have more impact on policy and practice. These include selecting issues of relevance to practitioners and decision-makers, communicating in concise and intelligible ways and interacting effectively with the people who need to use the research outcomes. Ways in which individuals, organisations and systems can enhance the impact of research in post-16 education and training have been the subject of a detailed study for the Learning and Skills Research Centre by a consortium of universities (LSRC, 2002). This analyses experience in social care, health and crime reduction as well as education to identify specific ways in which research evidence can be brought to bear on policy and practice. It offers advice on the most useful strategies for post-16 education and training and provides a theoretical model to aid understanding.

For individual practice-based researchers, as for research organisations, the key to securing impact is to clarify the purpose and objectives of a piece of research in collaboration with those who are expected to act on its outcomes. For example, where a teacher has discussed their proposed work with a decision-maker in their institution, and arrived at a design of value to both, the wider sense of ownership is more likely to lead to action as a consequence of the research. Such joint working can easily pose difficulties, for example on research whose outcomes might prove critical of institutional practice. But the development of strategies that both reflect the interests of the researcher and help the decision-maker make better judgements is what has to be confronted in helping applied research have greater impact.

Critical contribution of practitioners

There are several distinct ways in which practitioners need to participate in the overall process of research. Collectively, their views are vital in establishing agreement on the areas of practice that most urgently require research attention. Their practice-based knowledge is needed to design projects to ensure the methods are practicable and the outcomes applicable. Some practitioners also participate in data collection and analysis, others collaborate with full-time researchers in these tasks. It is at the interpretation stage, however, that the contribution of practitioners is indispensable. Experience of how change occurs in practice, how learners, teachers and managers operate in the day-to-day context is critical to effective interpretation and transformation of findings for practical use (Desforges, 2001).

Getting involved

We have now considered various ways in which practitioners can engage with research and various roles they may take up. It still remains to illustrate some ways in which this might happen in practice.

Individual teachers, guidance or learning support staff for example, may wish to investigate an aspect of their own practice systematically. A lecturer may wish to investigate the effect of different ways of marking students' work; a technician to compare different ways of using computerised data collection in practical classes; a marketing officer or team leader to analyse the profile of students enquiring about specific courses. Ways of collecting, analysing and interpreting data are considered throughout this book. Some wish to undertake these tasks on their own and to seek whatever time or funds they can by local negotiation. Others wish to develop their skills more systematically and to gain a qualification at the same time by undertaking a masters or doctoral degree. These are offered through universities and hence involve an academic approach to the study and assessment of research skills.

An alternative approach is to engage in networking with others with similar interests. Networks exist in, for example, professional associations such as the Institute of Physics or Institute of Linguists, through local authorities, regeneration partnerships or local projects. Some universities, particularly those that specialise in teacher training, organise practitioner networks. A specific network devoted to research in post-16 education and training is the Learning and Skills Research Network. It particularly encourages collaboration between the HE and Learning and Skills communities and is organised across England in regional groups (related networks exist in Scotland and Wales). Many networks serve to bring people together, but not specifically to undertake research. Good ideas, however, are often generated in such settings, which lead on to research activity.

The range of issues investigated by individual practitioners is well illustrated by examples of contributions to the *Learning and Skills Research* journal: learning styles amongst mature women returners, innovative curricula for reaching residents in a Newcastle housing estate, use of computers in maths teaching in a sixth form college. Typical themes for projects involving teams of practitioners are illustrated in the regional research scheme of the Learning and Skills Development Agency: collaboration for 14-16 education in the East Midlands, learner-centred curricula for adult basic skills in the North West, the effects of inspection on college staff in Yorkshire and Humberside.

In addition to those who are motivated towards research as a matter of personal interest, others may be led towards it as a way of addressing a problem they face in practice. Managers, team leaders, cross college coordinators and front line practitioners may become engaged in various ways. Most obviously, it may be of most value to read about research-based evidence that already bears on the problem. For this, the involvement of library and information staff can be helpful, as searching out and assessing the relevance of evidence is itself a skilled operation. Evidence needs to be judged in relation to the problem and judgements made about the precise point at which one's own investigation needs to pitch in. Based on this, a local investigation may be called for. To design an effective project, with achievable objectives and appropriate methods, a team approach is often advisable with links to a local university department or other sources of methodological experience.

Whilst the research community is beginning to consider ways of increasing the impact of its findings, the practice community is less advanced in considering ways of using them. Practitioners and decision-makers need time to engage with research. Libraries need resources to access research. Professional development programmes (and the standards that underpin them) need to encourage the use of research evidence in practice. These would be important elements in the professionalisation of education. Some advances have been made in school education through the work of the Teacher Training Agency, the General Teaching Council and the National College for School Leadership. The post-16 Leadership College will have a key role to play in this respect.

A culture of research

The involvement of individuals through networks such as the Learning and Skills Research Network has led to the development of conferences, seminars and publication formats that help people communicate about their work. Regional networks and local teams have felt encouraged by opportunities to run workshops and present papers at regional or national LSRN conferences and to write about their work or seek help through the *Learning and Skills Research* journal. From these, personal contacts are made, constructive criticism given and received and possibilities of collaboration explored. This socialising effect has proved important in a potentially lonely form of activity. Researchers from one community meet others from different ones, compare notes and build connections. This is practically important but also critical in breaking down misconceptions of the value of one another's contributions. In these ways a culture of research is beginning to emerge.

However, what lies ahead for all of us, is the growth of a broader culture of research that includes not only the many varieties of researchers, but also the teacher, trainer, adviser, librarian, manager, policy officer and employer. A culture that embraces the utilisation as well as the production of research will mark the arrival of a true education profession, at home equally with thought, knowledge and the development of practice.

Chapter 2
Changing policy issues facing the sector

Research does not exist in a vacuum, but is strongly affected by prevailing educational trends including policy-related issues.

An awareness of general policy issues is useful when practitioners make research proposals, for example to senior managers or funding bodies, to ensure the aims of research projects are linked to the international, national and local contexts of the time. Knowledge of specific trends in educational research in the learning and skills sector provides an important backdrop when framing research questions, and in developing the project's overall literature review.

Keeping up with rapid policy change

Research also needs to keep up with rapid policy change. Certain types of research that may have been useful in former times may no longer be appropriate. Sectoral trends swiftly change in an ongoing way. There is therefore a strong need for FE researchers to keep up with current sectoral knowledge and with cultural change. Research in the FE sector is also inevitably influenced by developments affecting research in HE. International, national and regional advancements in knowledge and research in the sciences, arts, in social policy, law, in health and in a number of vocationally specific industries also have a direct impact on FE research. Developments in healthcare practitioner research, for example, provide particularly useful models for FE.

This awareness of 'currency' in research will strongly determine its applicability and the impact of its findings. And yet research also affords a particular opportunity to build on the lessons of the past through reflection, and a responsibility to remind us of values and knowledge deriving from former eras.

Educational policy trends

Teachers have, essentially, always supported students to achieve 'success' and 'excellence', words much used in recent policy developments, which have for some years placed emphasis on every individual learner achieving their goals. Both 'success' and 'excellence' are highlighted in *Success for All* (DfES, 2002), and in the opening statement of the DfES strategy *Education and Skills: Delivering Results to 2006*:

> The Department for Education and Skills was established with the purpose of creating opportunity, releasing potential and achieving excellence for all. (DfES, 2002, page 1)

A trend announcing the potential for 'success for all' had begun some years earlier, as evidenced in the following statement from the DfEE's *Further Education for the New Millennium*. This document was the Labour government's response to *Learning Works* (1997) the report of the Further Education Funding Council's (FEFC) Committee on Widening Participation chaired by Baroness Helena Kennedy, indicating the government's commitment to fostering achievements in the wider population through education:

> This Government is committed to the establishment of a learning society in which all people have opportunities to succeed. (DfEE, 1998, Chapter 2, page 1)

Focusing on success for everyone emphasised the social inclusion and participation of 'all people', rather than just smaller numbers of a privileged elite, hence strongly adhering to principles of social justice and equality. This can be contrasted with the policies of earlier Conservative governments, for example, which focused more on fostering competition for the fittest to emerge and thrive in an increasingly privatised capitalist framework. The policies of John Major's government (1990-97) were more conciliatory than in the earlier Thatcherite Conservative government (1979-1990), widely seen as an era of aggressive controlling interventionism and monetarism. Nevertheless, in both of these governments, Tory principles of meritocracy in education were foregrounded, rather than those of social inclusion.

Linguistic trends reflect new policy developments

Political and cultural trends are more or less subtly reflected in the language in which policy is articulated, and in the terminology in which research questions are framed. For example, the most commonly used word to describe people who learn in the FE sector has subtly changed over a period of time from 'student' and 'client' to 'learner'. The use of the somewhat remote term 'client' possibly reflected the idea of seeing students in a professional consultative way, as if in a patient/doctor or legal business-like relationship. The influence of FEFC unit-based funding tariffs, competition between providers, an emphasis on 'Schedule 2' accredited courses and the achievement of national targets, increased use of marketing and a focus on business and financial imperatives strongly affected the FE sector under the FEFC in the period 1993-2001.

In taking colleges out of local authority control following the Further and Higher Education Act of 1992, the Conservative government fostered increased competition between colleges and schools, and reduced levels of regional and local collaboration. During this era, viewing students as 'clients' emphasised a professional business or caring contractual relationship between student and college, and was perhaps reflective of a tendency to regard students as numerical units to be counted in a scramble to reach targets, rather than as individuals with a capacity to learn.

By contrast, a more recent emphasis on the word 'learner' reflects the growth of the new Learning and Skills Council from 2001 onwards. The word 'learner' is an umbrella term for both 'students' and 'trainees': this mirrored the joining of 'education' with 'skills' in the Council. It also signified that teaching and learning-related matters were now again at the heart of the agenda for education, with a renewed emphasis on learners in the LSC manifesto. Increased regional and local collaboration between colleges, schools and training providers in lifelong learning partnerships also encouraged this emphasis on the 'voice of the learner'.

The teacher's role has been subtly changing for some time, from one in which teachers have acted as a fount of all knowledge instructing students, to the role of a guide, in which teachers support students to select and make use of appropriate opportunities and information that they need to learn for themselves. We can view education as either 'learning' or 'instruction' or both. These two views of education are not necessarily mutually incompatible. A dualistic view of education as *either* 'instruction by a teacher' *or* 'discovery by the learner' is not particularly helpful, since in the more balanced realities of the classroom, *both* exploration by learners and instruction by teachers is needed. The use of the term 'ILT' (for information and learning technology) in further education situated IT advances clearly in the context of this emphasis on learning using technology across the curriculum, rather than on the proliferation of hardware and software for its own sake. Teachers have also increasingly been regarded as 'facilitators' of 'blended learning' strategies enabling knowledge and skills acquisition by learners through a combination of face-to-face teaching with individual on-line learning approaches. This does not replace the role of instruction in transmitting knowledge, but complements and transforms it.

In vocational education, the word 'skills' has tended to replace an earlier emphasis on 'training' from the days of the former FEFC and Training and Enterprise Councils (TECs), from which the LSC and Employment Service (ES) took over work-based training at the end of March, 2001. This tendency to use the word 'skills' has arguably been influenced both by the LSC and by a growing awareness of the need to equip learners for new work patterns requiring an adaptable range of competences rather than to achieve one fixed qualification.

Re-branded concepts in educational policy reflect ongoing, periodically fashionable developments in governmental, political and sectoral thinking about education. Some recent examples of developing thinking from other fields of knowledge affecting the FE sector are in the use of terms such as 'diversity', 'leadership', 'partnership' and 'citizenship'. All of these reflect significant policy changes: on the one hand, in equal opportunities legislation and management, and on the other, in a growing awareness of the rights and duties of learners as citizens of the world operating in their own self-determined networks.

Overall DfES Strategy Framework to 2006

In December, 2002 the DfES published its strategic framework for the next four years, declaring that it had been established with the following three main purposes in mind:

- Creating opportunities for everyone to develop their learning;
- Releasing potential in people to make the most of themselves;
- Achieving excellence in standards of education and levels of skills.' (DfES, 2002)

These ambitious goals for improvement have been followed through with a wide range of policy developments and new funding proposals intended to use education as a mechanism to create a more 'inclusive' and 'prosperous' society. A strong 'improvement' agenda has been expressed in more detail in a number of specific policies explored below.

Lifelong learning policy developments

'Lifelong learning' has often been interpreted as an umbrella term for learning throughout life, encompassing education from 'cradle to grave'. The term is particularly associated with adult education and training, though is often also applied more generally to refer to education provision and initiatives in the learning and skills sector.

An emphasis on continuing education and the use of education for social reform purposes has been a significant feature of UK lifelong learning policy during the past decade. The term implies a recognition of a basic human entitlement to learning throughout life, not just during the years of statutory attendance in formal schooling. The term itself is of considerable social and political importance, and is part of the portfolio responsibility of the current (2003) government minister for higher education.

Hodgson (2000) traces the use of the term 'lifelong learning' from its early inception in the 1920s through the latter course of the twentieth century, outlining the 'Third Way' approach to education and training of the new Labour government 1997-2000. Hodgson draws attention to the new Labour government's first policy papers on lifelong learning in The *Learning Age* (1998), and *Learning to*

Succeed (1999). She notes both the advantages and tensions of a new strategic policy emphasis on central, regional and local planning and infrastructure for education in these documents and the government's subsequent creation of the LSC. Hodgson states that

> From an historical UK perspective, the concept of the Third Way could be seen as lying between Conservative free-market ideologies and Old Labour state ownership and regulation. This approach to lifelong learning remains largely voluntarist and gives considerable power to the market, but it is a market modified by local and national (and in the future possibly regional) planning and organizational steers. (Hodgson, 2000, p.14)

This 'voluntarist' nature of steering lifelong learning developments is perhaps logical, given that there remains a funding problem with the expansion of significantly enhanced financial support for adult continuing education for all citizens.

It's raining policy! A plethora of new initiatives

Given that the 1997-2003 government was elected on a Labour manifesto in 1997 that gave as its three key priorities 'education (HE), education (secondary), education (primary)', it is hardly surprising that a plethora of policy documents has emerged from government agencies about every sector and level of education in the years 1997-2003. The current government's commitment to this can perhaps be summed up in a statement made by Tony Blair in January, 2002 in a speech at the Centre of Life in Newcastle:

> We are driving the longest sustained period of investment in education for a generation, and by 2003-04 we will be spending a third more on it in real terms than in 1997. (Blair, 2002)

Perhaps not since the 1944 Education Act has there been such a commitment to expand, improve and invest in education. This 'driven' approach to educational 'improvement' in all its forms has primarily aimed to redress a divisive system of education that Claus Moser, Chairman of the Basic Skills Agency, summed up in the statement:

> For hundreds of years Britain has been brilliant at educating an elite: the problem is the other 80 per cent. (Sir Claus Moser, cited by Adonis, 1996)

Education policy 1997-2003 has therefore seemed to be the product of strongly committed and knowledgeable enthusiasts whose desire to take immediate action to redress past inequalities and problems has unleashed a tidal wave of initiatives, new funding, major changes, and strongly determined imperatives for improvements at every level. The enthusiastic, even visionary nature of the many education reforms in government and regional documents published in these years has been at one level inspiring, and at another somewhat intimidating. The proliferation of significantly new policies has imposed major challenges and many new targets for educational practitioners in FE sector and in the LSC in general.

There have been too many new policies rather than too few, and the remit of new policy documents has overlapped confusingly. In the rush of new policies, there has been little time to link them together and provide a consistent and comprehensive overview. An example of this relates to the division of education between 14-19 and post-16: policy documents overlapping in the 16-19 area have led to some confusions and difficulties at a local level of implementation.

A further difficulty has been that targets put forward with confidence have sometimes been too ambitious, lacking a basis in sound evidence and risking failure. An overload of changes leading to 'innovation fatigue' in provider institutions has sometimes resulted, so that practitioners have felt overwhelmed by the drive to change too much too soon. Confusion has also occurred from the fact that central versus regional and local implementation of policy developments has sometimes differed. There has therefore been tension between different levels and layers of responses to governmental proposals.

Major new funding initiatives 2002-6

The funding argument remains to be won that all citizens throughout their lives should always have an entitlement to full-time free education services at any level. Funding systems still favour full-time, younger students, and the full achievement of standard qualifications rather than smaller chunks of learning. Policy continues to prioritise statutory schooling and HE as the two leading education sectors. Nevertheless, strong support for lifelong learning policy initiatives, in particular by the current government, has enabled considerable progress to be made to develop FE-related lifelong learn-ing policy and practice in the period 1997-2003.

In December 2002 the learning and skills sector was allocated sub-stantial additional funds comprising major new governmental invest-ment to carry out new policy initiatives. The 2002/3 Education and Skills Secretary Charles Clarke announced unprecedented levels of new funding to support post-16 learning and skills in England at the national LSC 2002 annual conference. From April 2003 the LSC would receive a major increase in its national budget, allocating £8 billion in 2003-4 and £9.2 billion in 2005-6. In return for this new investment, Clarke expected far-reaching sustained improvements to the sector, plus a related significant increase in the UK's overall levels of attainment in education and skills.

LSC funding was therefore 'allocated on a something for something basis', to develop skills for the UK modern economy, through ex-tending and building on existing successful work in the LSC sector, such as 'bite-sized learning' initiatives, the Centres for Vocational Excellence (CoVE) programme and Employer Training Pilots. Additional funds would enable more funding flexibility, quality improvements and planning over a three-year span, enabling also transformations in the range, growth and quality of LSC educational provision. This major challenge to the sector was therefore aimed at simultaneously rewarding and stimulating unprecedented growth and improvements nationally and locally.

Need for long-term comprehensive planning and reflection

One major result of the publication of so many policy documents emerging swiftly, one on the heels of another, is that the need for longer-term comprehensive policy planning has not always been addressed. This in itself is nothing new: we are very familiar with short-termism, as it has been a feature of the education landscape for generations. What is necessary, however, is for longer-term com-prehensive planning that brings together and rationalises different policy initiatives, and takes into account more systematically the practical realities of difficulties faced on the ground by institutions and practitioners implementing multiple policy changes simul-taneously.

There is also a need for more time for reflection on the need for policy changes, and the ways in which to implement policy initiatives as they occur. To understand this, we need to begin to summarise an overall perspective on national policy proposals.

Different kinds of policy documents driving constant change

A variety of policy documents continuously affect FE practitioners. These include European policy documents, UK government, DfES and central Learning and Skills Council policy documents, regional policy statements and strategies from, for example, the local LSCs, regional and local governmental policies, and policy initiatives from our own and partner institutions. Each of these has a different kind and level of power to affect work in the FE sector, including the power of introducing funding, governance, management and quality monitoring regulations and procedures. If maximal power is seen to reside at the top of this policy food chain, in terms of national government legislation and major funding grants, then practitioners sometimes feel that they are at the bottom of the chain with the least power.

Top-down centrally driven policies have made constant demands on FE managers and practitioners to improve overall delivery in terms of leadership, governance, management, achievement, retention, teaching and learning quality, marketing, budgetary and staff management, staff development, data management, library, learning resources and IT provision, student support, careers guidance, estates management, facilities provision and college-wide leadership. Almost every aspect of FE delivery has been strongly affected by policy changes in the past decade, including those leading to wholesale national and local restructurings.

Underlying issues in national FE policy proposals

Some of the underlying issues in national policy proposals as they affect education and skills in the FE sector are the following:

- legislative changes in the UK and EU

- economic issues, both national and international

- changes in government, in leadership and ministerial strategic priorities

- changes in the relationship of education with other home affairs issues

- competitive influences in foreign, national and regional affairs

- structural organisational change in central, regional and local governance

- quality performance of education and skills institutions

- changes in curriculum, accreditation and qualifications systems

- staffing issues, including changes in personnel, employment law and union issues

- trends in the student population, including financial issues

- trends in technological and communications developments

- trends in diversity and equal opportunities, including gender, race and disability

- trends in sectoral industrial and economic affairs

- the influence of other, related national and local policy documents and initiatives

These influences are too vast in their complexity and implications for FE policy and practice to analyse them in detail here in relation to any one particular policy document. We do not have space to analyse all of the implications of all policies affecting FE during these years, but suggest at the end of this chapter some useful starting points to learn from the work of those who have contributed to and are currently developing such analyses.

The incorporation of FE into the FEFC lasted a mere nine years before colleges again faced a new leadership in the LSC. Although many of the changes and policy directives during that time have been beneficial, and certainly all would appear at face value to have been well-meaning, the overall picture is one of constant top-down imposition of more or less radical change, in a situation in which organisations themselves are constantly restructuring, often in reaction to policy change. Much of this has been formulated without the benefit of research evidence involving practitioners. Instead of a clear pool in which to carry out work as practitioners, we therefore always seem to be operating in an environment constantly raining with new policies.

Framework for examining educational policy

Colleges have responded in different ways to such changes and policy imperatives, some very successfully, some less so. A number of policy changes have been very beneficial, and some less so. Essentially, however, state education in FE institutions, by contrast with private education, is both policy-driven and policy-dominated. It is therefore helpful to examine the ways in which such policies influence us, and the ways in which we can formulate our own responses to participate effectively in ongoing evidence-based policy development.

Scott (2000) provides a useful framework for examining educational policy, noting that policy documents can be regarded as texts of many different kinds:

> A policy text may be: prescriptive or non-prescriptive, ideologically explicit or opaque, generic or directed, single-authored or multiple-authored, diagrammatic or written, referenced to other texts or free of such references, coherent or fragmented, and have a wide or narrow focus.

> In order to critically read a policy text, the reader or practitioner needs to understand their reading as constructed by these various devices. They also need to locate their reading within the policy process itself (Scott, 2000, p. 21).

To locate our readings of policy within the policy process is to gain an authentic voice for practitioners. Reflective awareness through policy analysis can help us in this process, and prevent us from being tossed powerlessly in different directions every few years by the tides of unrelenting change.

Reflexivity and metacognitive awareness in policy analysis

In the natural world, it can be difficult for organisms to be aware of all the features of their environment. Humans can, however, with some effort, use strategies and develop abilities to help them increase awareness of their environment. Two such abilities are *reflexivity* (thinking about thinking) and *metacognitive awareness* (knowledge of the ways in which we learn).

The concept of *reflexivity* (Giddens, 1984) meaning the ability pro-actively to reflect, analyse and self-critically vocalise our own reflections while maintaining a critical awareness of the nature of culture and society around us, is useful for researchers. Maintaining a critical distance from policy proposals, rather than accepting all policies wholesale, enables us to ensure that the locus of control for our work stays more in our power.

The concept of *metacognitive awareness* meaning knowledge of our own learning processes can also be developed to scrutinise our cognitive capacities to learn and make use of opportunities available in the environments around us. To improve our own learning skills can help us distinguish the ways in which we react to policy. We can also learn about and develop our capacity to discriminate between things that are of lasting value from those which are transient, in policy terms. Such skills can also help us differentiate between good and poor quality in policy implementation: sometimes a differentiating process that we find difficult.

It's useful, therefore, to employ reflexivity and metacognitive awareness to examine the current policy trends that surround us, in awareness that these trends are changing rapidly every day. By the time we read this page again, everything in the policy environment will again be changing.

The development of reflexivity and metacognitive awareness can therefore help us build our own local umbrellas and irrigation systems to cope with a constant rain of changes in the policy environment.

Analysing policy documents as textual 'powerstories'

As we have noted from Scott (2000) above, practitioners benefit from recognising that educational policy initiatives can be read as texts, like any others, that are capable of being analysed and interpreted in a variety of ways. Policy documents are not transparently neutral. They are also neither author-free nor value-free entities, no matter how much such documents appear to be written on tablets of stone.

Policy documents derive from particular viewpoints of the government and ministers of the day, and are in fact 'powerstories' interpreting current educational facts and situations to put forward specific viewpoints for particular purposes. The reason these documents are significantly more powerful than most other 'stories' about education is that often they may lead to large changes through legislation, financial allocations, and changes in national governance or sectoral organisation. These changes may be economic, political, social and/or governmental. Policy documents are inevitably value-laden. It is empowering for researchers to analyse and critique these documents to establish the basis of the values and the accuracy of the information that has shaped their authorship.

In analysing educational policy documents, Scott (2000) models the policy process as: (a) centrally controlled, or (b) pluralist or (c) fragmented and multi-directed. The most empowering model for FE practitioners amongst these would be model (c) policy processes, in which there is an opportunity for feedback and for the results of practical modifications to be included in an ongoing policy-making process. This tends to be a democratic and participative model adopted in the implementation of some more recent governmental policies, which have been openly and widely disseminated, with opportunities for feedback and for changes to be made. Though some are cynical about the real power of respondents to change the basic thrust of policies, some recent policy modifications have been made which indicate a potential for practitioner voices to be heard. It is clear, also, that recent trends in government thinking indicate a willingness to engage with the lessons derivable from practical research.

Gap between educational policy and evidence from practitioners

A key factor in the analysis of policy is to determine the extent to which it is driven by evidence-based research based on practitioner knowledge. In effect, it has often seemed as if little evidence has been used to drive forward educational policy during the past decades.

An example of this is in the development of GNVQ programmes to replace National Diploma (ND) and Higher National Diploma (HND) programmes in FE colleges in the 1990s. Significant levels of popularity existed for ND and HND programmes during the 1990s, especially amongst employers for certain high quality vocational industry-standard courses, such as some of those in media or engineering. The introduction of the GNVQ therefore came as a surprise and disappointment to many in the FE sector, who continued to retain their long-standing ND and HND courses, and still do.

When the GNVQ was replaced with Advanced level vocational courses, this policy development also failed to take sufficient account of the evidence that many colleges, having by this time adjusted to the requirement to grow new GNVQs, now had developed GNVQ work to high levels, and did not want to get rid of GNVQ courses entirely. This is merely one example of the way in which top-down policy initiatives have sometimes ignored the experience and knowledge of 'what works' on the ground. There are countless others, including relative difficulties and practical problems that emerged during the implementation of policy proposals on curriculum 2000, key skills, individual learning accounts, New Deal, A/AS levels, Management Information Systems (MIS) developments, and a range of other initiatives.

Growth of evidence-informed education

Partly as a result of dilemmas of this kind, there has been in the UK for at least a decade a growing demand for more substantial links to be established between the evidence of research and the development of new social science policy. The creation of the Centre for Evidence-informed Education Policy and Practice Information (EPPI) at the London University Institute of Education in 1993, together with the development of the LSRN and LRSC traced in this book, are two indications of this trend, which has strongly affected both practice and policy in health and education.

A further indication of this emerging trend can be noted from the 2002 National Foundation for Educational Research (NFER) Council Address given by Dr John Dunford, General Secretary of the Secondary Heads Association (Dunford, 2002). Arguing that there needs to be a significantly stronger connection between research evidence and government educational policy, Dr Dunford commented humorously,

Why, then, is government policy so often introduced without any basis in research? Governments, of course, are always in a hurry. They have three time scales: immediately, next year, and after the next election (Dunford, 2002).

A more recent tendency for the DfES to call together evidence from practitioners to inform policy in, for example, regional workshops, is a refreshing sign of change in this area. However, although the generally weak UK link between education policy formation and research evidence is at the time of writing being addressed more systematically than in previous decades, there remains still a very considerable gap between evidence and policy.

Finding an authentic voice as a practitioner

It is hard for practitioner-researchers to comment in a responsible, proactive way on governmental, regional and local policies. We remember the story of a young undergraduate studying philosophy, who, faced with the works of Plato, Aristotle, Marx and Hegel and needing to write an essay about all of these, commented, 'Where do I start? These guys were world-class experts, famous throughout time – I'm just me, and I don't know anything!'

Practitioners have important perspectives to contribute to education policy. The voices of those on the ground or 'at the coalface' teaching in the classroom or working in support areas are perhaps more authentic than any others in education, and should be heard. This vocalisation process needs to take account of the different ways in which FE institutions respond to policy initiatives. We need, in short, to have faith in the importance of the practitioner viewpoint, and to develop confidence in the ongoing value of this.

Typology of FE responses to policy

We suggest a model for FE institutional responses to education policy, drawing upon Scott (2000), who cites Saunders' (1985) typology of schools' unexpected responses to the Technical and Vocational Educational Initiative (TVEI) in the 1980's, classifying three basic responses as: *adaptive extension, accommodation* and *containment.*

We propose a new typology of institutional and individual responses to policies for FE below, suggesting the following four kinds of res-

resistant: blocks change	accommodatory: swallows up
responds unthinkingly to policy with cynical, tired or inert rejection of policy changes: attempts to ignore, block, subvert or hijack new policy with little attempt to investigate if policies will work in practice	responds thoughtfully, but waters down attempts to investigate if policies will work by adjusting policy to fit in with local situation, new policies are swallowed up, achieving little or no real impact long-term
- leads to dangerous lack of compliance in response to new policy, to crisis management longer-term, probable staff resistance from mismanagement, and failing inspection grades.	- leads to some practical policy results and little staff resistance but lack of real impact or change from new policy, a self-enclosed, empowered institution misses out on invigorating new initiatives
over-compliant: rushes in	**reflexive: reaches balance**
responds unthinkingly to policy and implements swiftly: little attempt to investigate whether policies will work in practice	responds thoughtfully and enthusiastically to new policy: implements a planned proactive consultative investigation adjusted to local situation to see if policies will work in practice
- leads to immediate multiple policy adoptions, but probable staff resistance from overload of changes and crisis management, with loss of self- empowerment and institutional identity longer-term	- can lead to quality long-term results, empowered staff, and a sense of institutional pride in tailoring policy to fit effectively and achieve local success

Figure 2.1: A typology of FE institutional and practitioner responses to policy documents

ponses: resistant, *over-compliant, accommodatory*, and *reflexive*. We examine the range of these different possible responses to policy in Figure 2.1.

The *resistant* response is one that rejects new policy. This may be the intuitive response of those who are tired, cynical or inert as a result of the plethora of changes that have affected FE during the past years. It may also be the personal reaction of some practitioner-teachers who have previously been required to carry forward too many changes too quickly with few resources and no support.

Resistance tends to be an emotional unthinking response rather than one that is reflective. This kind of response automatically rejects new policy without thought. It is a dangerous attitude to take in terms of adaptability to change, as it fails to take account of the requirements of new policy changes, and the implications, for example, of new curricular, funding and quality demands. Nevertheless, it exists as a real response to change and may sometimes be the first reaction of some practitioners before they develop more adaptive reactions to new policy requirements.

The uncritically *over-compliant* response is one that accepts new policy documentation too quickly, with or without enthusiasm and in a driven manner, lacking reflective analysis of the real significance of the impact of policy changes. Practitioners and managers in FE are sometimes so busy with the immediate demands of responding to problems with delivery that this type of response may sometimes seem sensible, providing the easiest way of coping. We suggest, however, that overall this approach, while pragmatic and adaptive in responding to demand, is ultimately unproductive.

We suggest that this kind of response can lead to relative 'crisis management', a lack of institutional ownership of new policy, and a feeling of being driven too much from the outside. If staff are not fully consulted and involved in the processes of policy implementation, this kind of over-compliant, unthinking response can lead to feelings of disempowerment in practitioners, resentment and overload from too many changes too soon and too often. Nevertheless, it is a more responsible attitude to take to policy change than the 'resistant' one, it is enthusiastic about change, and willing to jump in to implement new initiatives vigorously and energetically.

The *accommodatory* response incorporates a usefully reflective attempt to ensure the feasibility of policy implementation. However, this kind of response tends to water down large-scale incorporation of new policies by absorbing these into the maintenance of the status quo. It is therefore ultimately a thoughtful, but more or less tacitly resistant and over-controlling approach to new initiatives, giving an overall sense of not being driven enough from the outside. Being somewhat over-cautious, it is diametrically opposite to the 'over-compliant' response. This may sometimes be the response of controlling managers who maintain quality, well-maintained institutions but are dismissive of proposed new policy changes, and more or less resistant to learn from them. This kind of reaction is a good quality reaction to policy in a number of respects, in that it does responsibly if reluctantly take on board new policies in a limited way, and reflectively analyses these. However, as a response it tends to lack genuine enthusiasm for new ideas, and may often be marked by a degree of institutional arrogance. This limits it from being a fully effective way of dealing with new policies.

The *reflexive* response reacts thoughtfully and enthusiastically to new policy, but implements this in a planned consultative investigation adjusted to the local situation to see if policies will work in practice. This kind of response to policy is excellent, leading to long-term high quality results, empowered staff, and a sense of institutional pride in tailoring policy to fit effectively within the college. This is a response utilising both the reflexivity of research processes, and the practical feasibility deriving from practitioner consultation and ownership, to make the institution into a unique place with its own voice and distinct culture.

These four different kinds of possible responses by FE institutions, including managers and practitioners, to new policy initiatives and documents, are just some suggested likely reactions. These are not definitive or complete as a range of responses, but rather suggested markers along a continuum of possible reactions to policy. We suggest that in the development of an authentic voice for practitioner-researchers to respond to and initiate policy, this typology of potential responses may be useful in analysing an institutional and individual place in this continuum.

The key point is for practitioners to realise that we have some potential power to shape and adjust policy to fit our own situation more closely. In short, we can be proactive rather than reactive. This realisation can in more or less subtle ways change the balance of power in the policy-making process. Instead of blindly rejecting or wholesale accepting new policy, instead of watering down initiatives defensively or reluctantly to accommodate policy change in only minor ways, we can *both* enthusiastically *and* critically evaluate new initiatives.

This frees us to respond fully to new policies in an authentic way, using reflective analysis and research evidence to tailor changing policies to fit our own, unique, personally worked and shaped best practice models. The lessons of making proactive responses, of valuing and using our own internal freedoms to empower our choices, are applicable to our work. The knowledge of our ability to respond to policy initiatives in a personally-selected proactive and reflexive way is therefore ultimately the route to empowerment as a practitioner-researcher.

Finding out more:

Hodgson, A. (2000) *Policies, Politics and the Future of Lifelong Learning*, Series: The Future of Education from 14+ London: Kogan Page

Hodgson, A. and Spours, K. (1999) *New Labour's Educational Agenda: Issues and Policies for Education and Training*, Series: The Future of Education from 14+ London: Kogan Page

Department for Education and Employment (1998) *The Learning Age: Further Education for the New Millennium* London: DfEE

Department for Education and Skills (2002a) *Success for All* London: DfES

Department for Education and Skills (2002b) *Education and Skills: Delivering results to 2006* London: DfES

Further Education Funding Council (1997) *Learning Works* (Report of the FEFC's Committee on Widening Participation in Further Education, chaired by Baroness Kennedy). Coventry: FEFC

Chapter 3
Framing questions of research: developing professional knowledge

It is Friday afternoon, the last week of term and Desmond has been asked to take the portfolio building session for the electrical engineering course as his colleague has gone home with flu. Desmond knows about portfolio building, he knows about electrical engineering, and he is just about to find out what it is like combining the two with a group of people who would rather be anywhere else than in the college on the last Friday of term! Yet Desmond turns the session into one that is fun, and where the learners gain a lot. How did he do that?

The answer lies in the fact that Desmond has spent years working on a voluntary basis with disaffected teenagers in his local youth club. He combines his knowledge of working with young people, gained informally, with his vocational knowledge of electrical engineering, and his academic knowledge of using portfolios to help learners identify their achievements. Desmond, therefore, has a lot of professional knowledge that he has brought to bear to the new situation in which he finds himself.

Professional knowledge is gained in a number of ways. Most people who work in further education have spent many years studying their specialist area, either academically or vocationally. They then practice this knowledge daily. Each time a new situation arises, they learn from it, applying their previous knowledge and skill and identifying what works and what doesn't.

Different kinds of knowledge

Eraut (1994, 1998) has studied how people develop their professional knowledge and competence. He argues that there are different types of knowledge. The first is the type found in books and taught explicitly in formal learning contexts. This type of knowledge he calls *propositional*. This kind of knowledge has concepts, generalisations and principles of practice.

There is another type of knowledge that is far less explicit, which is *personal* knowledge. Such knowledge arises from interpreting personal experiences and is therefore impressionistic in nature. Our knowledge about any context builds up as we gain more experience. Such knowledge draws upon propositional knowledge but also upon experience.

A third type of knowledge is *process* knowledge. This type of knowledge is often gained from working with people. When we want to find out about something, we often ask other people. We know, therefore, where to go for advice and to acquire and give information. It is a bit like the car advert where someone asks a question and the response is 'I don't know but I know someone who can'. Who do you go to when you want to find out how to make your computer respond? Who do you ask about the latest management committee decisions? Who knows about the best place to get a decent cup of coffee in the college? This type of knowledge is not written down, it is word of mouth. We usually find out that some people are a great store of knowledge; caretakers and receptionists are examples of people who know a lot about 'the way things are around here' simply because they work across the college and meet all kinds of people.

Explicit and tacit knowledge

Eraut further expands these three forms of knowledge by characterising them as *explicit* or *tacit*. Explicit knowledge is what is 'out in the open'. It is often written down and codified knowledge. The second form of knowledge is often not articulated at all. We can learn things explicitly formally in classrooms and through books, and we learn them informally, through dialogue with our colleagues. Tacit knowledge is that which we develop without being aware of it. It is akin to the idea of becoming unconsciously competent. If you remember learning to ride a bike, you may also recall having to concentrate very hard. Once you had acquired this skill, you could ride along a road without thinking about what you were doing. Tacit knowledge is like that. You perform a huge number of complex operations every day, and you would find it almost impossible to explain to someone else how you did most of them.

Other ways to express this knowledge is knowing how and knowing that (Ryle 1949). Attwell, Jennes and Tomassini (1997), expand upon this idea by suggesting there are four different types of knowledge:

- Knowing what: facts, information

- Knowing why: scientific knowledge

- Knowing how: skills

- Knowing who: social skills, who to ask

We can see that knowledge is not a simple phenomenon.

If we want to find out whether what we know and do is effective, or indeed we want to test knowledge, then we need a way to draw upon the tacit as well as explicit nature of that knowledge. If there are colleagues who are successfully enabling people to learn effectively, then surely we would want to find out the exact nature of what they do which works so well. Research, therefore, in further education should draw upon the wealth of professional knowledge that resides within the people who work in the sector.

Knowledge and truth

We need to take a step back and examine more fundamental questions about knowledge. Philosophers have been challenged for centuries over questions about what we know, how we can know it. Plato argued that we cannot know the truth, but that we only can appreciate the shadows of truth, as though we lived in a cave and could not see the physical things themselves, only shadows of these things. Centuries later, Descartes famously said 'I think, therefore I am' acknowledging that we are conscious of our existence and the world around us.

Empiricists have had great fun arguing about how we can know anything from our senses, when we can be so easily deceived by them.

A stick in water looks bent because of refraction, yet our senses are overriden by our knowledge of the world which tells us that sticks do not change shape.

Why is this important for research? If we can't trust our senses, then how can we ever set out to learn something about the world, in other words, how can we undertake research? In books about research methods, you will read about the issue of knowledge, and how it is constructed. We simply cannot go off and undertake research if we have not at least appreciated that the kind of knowledge that we are using and seeking does not have any inherent 'truth' and is much debated by philosophers, scientists and social scientists.

Let us look at an example. We know that water boils at one hundred degrees centigrade because we have thermometers that tell us so. We also know that it does this only at sea level, because we have tried boiling water up mountains, and the water boils at lower temperatures there where the air pressure is lower. We know these things because we make experiments. We try and keep as many variables (factors which may change the situation) as constant as possible so that we find out the effect of the one variable we are interested in measuring. Everything in this situation is based on a notion that there are physical laws that can be identified and we achieve this by measurement using our senses.

The approach just described is a scientific approach. We are so used to scientific knowledge these days that we forget that it has only taken precedence in the last three centuries. The scientific approach to knowledge is based on the conviction that laws can describe, predict and explain phenomena. All we have to do is to keep measuring our variables, and we will be able to create laws for all phenomena. Our knowledge is therefore gradually increased as we conduct more experiments, and we test out our ideas from hunches, or hypotheses, to see if they stand up to scrutiny. Hypotheses are often expressed in 'if then' statements, such as '*if* you heat water to one hundred degrees centigrade, *then* it will boil'.

Imagine we have a group of learners in a hairdressing salon. Perhaps we want to find out if a new learning resource is better than the one we currently use. We cannot put them into an experimental situation in the same way, because we are dealing with people. We could divide them into two groups, and give one the new resource and one the other. There are ethical reasons why we cannot do this, but there are practical reasons, too. If one resource is better than the other, we have prevented half our learners from benefiting from it. As we have only tried out one resource, we do not know if our groups are different. Perhaps all the learners who are experiencing difficulty with the subject could be in the group that gets the old resource. In this case, any difference in performance may be due to the differences between the two groups, and not the difference between the two types of resource.

It is not clear that we could find laws that predict, describe and explain why people behave consistently. People tend not to behave in the same way, even if we could hold as many variables constant as possible. It would be difficult for us to find out that if we do one thing, another will happen. However, this is not to say that we should not try to think in these terms. We can still test out a new teaching resource. We could have a hunch, or hypothesis that states '*if* we provide learners with a new, interactive web based programme, *then* they will perform better in the projects.' The trouble is, we have so many different factors involved in the situation, we cannot claim that we have found such a law for all possible events in the future. We cannot predict, and we probably cannot explain either. We can simply describe.

Another way of approaching the knowledge question is to examine how people think. Instead of trying to create laws, would it not be better to find out what people *experience*?

Paradigms

When scientific approaches to discovering knowledge operate, there are set rules about what we should do. We need to identify a hypothesis, undertake an experiment which measures our phenomenon whilst holding other variables constant, and then we analyse our results and decide if we have evidence for our hypothesis or not. Everything we do must follow such a regime, so that others can come along and replicate our experiments to further test them, or to try a similar experiment holding a different set of variables constant.

This approach to doing things, is more than abiding by a set of rules. It relates to a view of how the world operates. This kind of 'world view' is called a paradigm.

Centuries ago, in Europe, the scientific paradigm was not accepted. This is because it contradicted ideas about the position of the earth, and more particularly, the role of God in controlling the world. When one person began to challenge the notion that the earth was not the centre of the universe, or that the sun and moon went around the earth, he was subject to imprisonment for challenging the accepted 'world view'. This person was Galileo. As a result of pain-stakingly observing the heavens, helped by the new invention of a more powerful optical device, the telescope, Galileo eventually provided enough evidence that contradicted the previous view and the new 'paradigm' began to take hold.

Thomas Kuhn (1970) argued that over time, the paradigm of the day becomes challenged when a few people begin to think differently and challenge the current view of the world. This paradigm shift is difficult for many people within a particular community to accept. Eventually, enough people are prepared to take on the new paradigm and they begin operating within the rules of this new paradigm or world view. A paradigm is *not* simply a way of doing things. It is a way of looking at the world and operating within it.

The scientific paradigm has become challenged in the last century by a number of influential theorists and researchers. They have argued that we cannot know the world by relying on our senses and taking measurements to create laws. We have to accept that there are different perceptions and perspectives and we must find ways to shed light on the way people think and behave. This is a completely different way of looking at the world, indeed, it is a paradigm shift. This new paradigm, called the *illuminative* paradigm, really does try to shed light. It is 'incommensurate' with the scientific paradigm, because it accepts that there are multiple perspectives, something the scientific paradigm cannot allow.

When we decide what kind of question we are asking in our own research, we do need to think about the paradigm we are operating in. Are we trying to find universal laws, or are we trying to throw some light on a particular issue? Do we want to gain multiple perspectives, indeed, do we even consider that these are a possibility?

Quantitative and qualitative methods of research

If a paradigm is an overall way of looking at the world, then within it, there are methods of finding out about that world. Research methods are often divided into two neat groups, quantitative and qualitative methods. Although this is too simplistic and misleading, the distinction is often used when discussing approaches to research.

Counting numbers and capturing words

As you can imagine, data comes in many forms. If you want to know how many people pass examinations, your data is numerical. If you want to know how they felt about taking their examinations, you could ask for people's views and your richest source of data would therefore be verbal. There are two main types of data, *quantitative* and *qualitative*, and each requires different ways of analysis. Quantitative analyses basically work with numbers. If you are in the scientific paradigm, then you will want to measure your phenomena. This automatically creates a need for using numbers and your approach, therefore, is a quantitative one.

Qualitative data is not, as the name might suggest, of higher quality than quantitative data. It simply means that the data is not in the form of numbers but in different formats such as words, or pictures, or sounds, and is usually gathered by different methods from those used to collect quantitative data. Such data is not easily converted into numbers, but can be. How you analyse qualitative data is just as difficult to do as analysing numerical data, and is often more so.

Approaches to research and research tools

Blaxter, Hughes and Tight (1996) have a really helpful way of describing using research in education. They suggest there are paradigms, within which are approaches to conducting research. These approaches will be quantitative or qualitative in nature. Within approaches, there are very specific tools. If an approach is an umbrella, the tools are the spokes. Research methods are the tools.

If you ask people to give a rating on items in a questionnaire (more of which in chapter 9), then you immediately have a method which

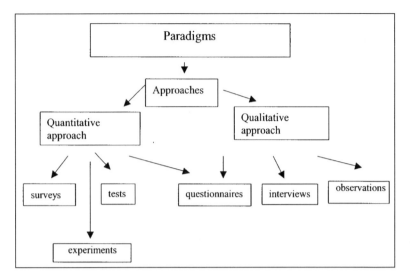

Figure 3.1: Framing questions of knowledge

yields quantitative data, and arguably, your method therefore is quantitative in nature. However, you may also have a section on your questionnaire for more 'open' questions, where people write in their own ideas and comments. Now you have qualitative data, so questionnaires are also tools for qualitative research methods, too.

It is crucial that you do not develop the idea that all quantitative methods are scientific, all qualitative methods are illuminative, or even vice versa, that scientific methods are only quantitative and illuminative methods are only qualitative. This splitting methods into two main camps has created one of the most futile debates in research methodology.

Framing research questions

A fundamental part of any research process is to decide exactly what you want to find out, and why. In the same way that people think they have one problem but on talking about it to colleagues, they discover that the nature of the problem is something entirely different, so it is with research questions. If you have an issue, it helps if you set out everything about that issue, perhaps in a 'spidergram' or 'exploded thematic chart'. You may begin to find that one theme or aspect is dependent upon another, or that one area is of more importance to you, or more possible for you to investigate.

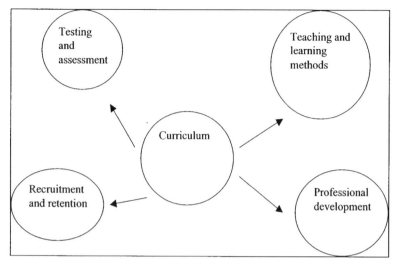

Figure 3.2: Spidergram of themes

Grounded theory

We often ask people to think carefully about their research question before they launch into setting up their methodology and gathering their data. Not all research must start with a well defined question or hypothesis. Glaser and Strauss (1967) created a research approach called grounded theory, where they proposed that we should allow our examination of events and situations to create theories, rather than to start off with a particular idea which is subsequently tested by research. This approach is particularly appropriate when we are trying to examine an undefined area.

Imagine that you want to find out what it is like being a disabled teenager attending a large mixed FE college after leaving a special school. You do not know what the important issues are, and in a way, it is better not to prejudge them, as you cannot know a disabled person's experience personally if you are able bodied. Your understanding may be derived from empathy, but not from personal experience, (unless you have been injured, or incapacitated temporarily during awareness raising professional development sessions). Grounded theory would allow the researcher to record any number of events, interview people, observe behaviour and so forth, without starting off with a list of ready made questions. The data would then be analysed by placing into themes or categories.

Once these emerging themes have been identified, the data is re-visited to test whether these categories are valid and reliable. It is only when the data has yielded the categories exhaustively, can the theory begin to emerge. The approach does not set out with specific questions already framed, but lets the data gathering process lead to theorising and developing hypotheses afterwards. At this point, the new hypotheses which have been generated can be tested to identify if they are valid, and applicable across a range of contexts. Bloomer (1997) adopted this approach in his investigation of the social conditions of studentship in post-16 programmes of learning. Grounded theory is a valuable approach but requires great skill, particularly in the analysis of data and generating theory arising from the analysis.

Defining aims and objectives

Let us return to our original example, Desmond and a group of reluctant learners on a Friday afternoon. Desmond is doing a Certificate in Education course. He has been asked to devise a project that investigates how to facilitate learning. He realises that he is increasingly being asked to work with younger age groups, including 14 year olds who no longer attend their local secondary school.

Desmond's first thought is that he has to create a project, undertake it, and write a 10,000 word project report within four months. Naturally, his priority is to think of what he can achieve within the timescale. This is a very sensible starting point. Desmond has not been given a 'blue skies' remit, where he can think of something to do with no fixed timescale, unlimited resources, and an open choice about the subject to investigate. Desmond has limited time, virtually no additional resources, and a clear set of criteria against which his project will be judged. These constraints are actually very helpful in enabling Desmond to decide on a project. There is no point trying to do something which requires a long time to set up, and a high level of resourcing.

A good place to start in such a situation is to ask what would help improve the teaching and learning situation. As Desmond knows that he has an increasing responsibility for teaching disaffected young people, then would it not be a good idea to find more ways to work with them? This begins to create a fuzzy idea. Desmond now needs

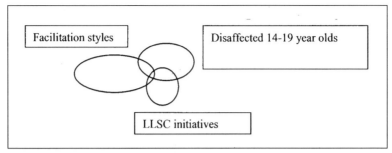

Figure 3.3: Venn diagram showing three overlapping issues

to identify the issues that relate to this situation. One way to do this is to think of the main idea as a circle, with overlapping circles for linked issues, often expressed as a Venn Diagram.

Alternatively, each circle could relate to a number of other issues, or fields, which may begin to link with each other, therefore creating a network.

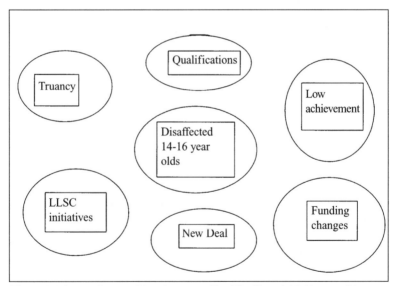

Figure 3.4: Issues for consideration regarding Disaffected 14-16 year olds

Once Desmond has created his image, or list of all the factors and issues that are relevant to his original idea, he can start deciding which he must include in his research, and which are either not relevant, not central, or simply impossible to deal with within the constraints of his research brief. This is a 'focusing down' approach, which begins to isolate the main issue.

Desmond has decided that he wants to look at the perceptions of young people who are sent to the college from school, compared with young people who are sent to the college from New Deal. He is therefore already creating a research question which begins to suggest a research approach to help him answer his questions. But what are his questions?

- Is there a difference between the motivation of young people who attend the college from school or New Deal programmes?

- Why do young people attend college?

- Do young people have different levels of attendance at college?

- What kinds of patterns of attendance exist for young people attending college?

- What are the barriers to learning experienced by young people?

Each of these questions is perfectly acceptable as a research question, but some of them are more likely to lead to useful project outcome within the remit that Desmond has.

Desmond decides that the question that is most likely to help him is the last one. If he knows about the barriers affecting young people's learning, he is more likely to be able to do something about it.

So we now have a research question. Desmond has to choose which research approach will help him begin to answer his question. His question is not obviously located in a scientific paradigm or an illuminative one. He could use datasets about attendance, postcode analyses and achievement levels. He could talk to young people. He could even ask young people to record their own ideas on video. Desmond's question is not yet fully refined. He needs to break it down further, and by doing so, begin to create some aims and objectives for his research. Desmond redefines his aim as:

> To investigate the barriers to learning experienced by 14-19 year olds who are potential students at Good Hope College.

Note how precise this aim is now. There is a specific target group, situated in one geographic location. What kind of barriers is Desmond trying to identify? There are structural barriers, and attitudinal ones. What information already exists that Desmond can call upon? By thinking through these questions, Desmond can decide on a much tighter framework for his project.

As there is data about travel to study, costs of study and recruitment and retention rates for 16 year olds in the college, Desmond decides to use this information as a test bed for investigating the attitudinal barriers. So he has pinned his question down to the attitudinal barriers that affect 14-16 year olds. How will he answer his research question?

• By analysing existing data on recruitment, retention and achievement for 14-16 year olds in the catchment area of the college

• By interviewing a sample of learners from each age group who attend college

• By interviewing a sample of learners from each group who do not attend college but who are at school, or who attend a local youth centre.

These can now become his objectives:

• To examine existing data on recruitment, retention and achievement for 14-16 year olds in the catchment area of the college

• To interview a sample of learners from each age group who attend college currently

• To interview a sample of learners from each age group who do not attend college currently, in the local school and local youth centre.

What will be the result of Desmond's investigation? It is very helpful to identify the outcomes of any research project, so that you can check that your research idea, your strategy and the data you collect will actually provide you with the outcomes you seek.

Desmond wants as an outcome a list of barriers to learning, attitudinal and structural that exist for young people, so that he can make a set of recommendations for action within the college, and a staff development strategy for enabling his colleagues to work more effectively with this target group.

This means that Desmond will produce a piece of small-scale research that will be of benefit to a wide audience, which creates strategies for action based upon research evidence, and which can lead to further testing as the strategies are implemented.

Choosing research methods

Now Desmond needs to capture this as a project proposal. Chapter 5 will discuss how this can be done. The next chapters will help you be in a position, like Desmond, to create a research proposal, undertake research, analyse your findings and discuss their implication.

Finding out more

A general introduction to research methods in education can be found in:

Cohen, L., Manion, L., and Morrison, K. (2000) *Research methods in education*

For paradigms and philosophy of science

Chalmers, A.F. (1982) *What is this thing called Science?* Buckingham: Open University Press

Section Two
Finding out the main issues

Chapter 4
Small-scale research: action research and reflective practice

Small-scale research in the context of further education

In developing an 'empowerment' model for practitioners in further education research, we draw on the different roles staff hold in the FE sector throughout this book. The large number of FE, adult, training and HE colleges in the UK has enabled the formation of national, regional and local communities of professional practice to develop in specialist areas of knowledge. Examples of these can be found in the current FE principal and senior management networks, FE specialist teacher groups, research networks, human resources, IT, MIS, learning resources, library, administrative and other professional groupings that exist across the UK and regularly meet or are in contact via email discussion groups. These groups are often peer-group networks providing friendly support and help, sharing information, collaborating for problem-solving and generally providing a rich source of professional expertise that can be invaluable to staff in the sector.

The concept of 'reflective practice' is intimately bound up with the specialist roles that such staff hold in colleges, and the kinds of professional knowledge and skills they develop and share as 'communities of practice'.

Reflective practice

As we noted in chapter 3, people who work in further education colleges have a wealth of professional knowledge. We also argued that this knowledge is often tacit, unexplained and difficult to articulate. The problem with such knowledge is that it cannot be easily tested. So, one danger is that ideas and practices can become stultified, and 'taken for granted', resulting in resistance to change. A way forward is to be open to our assumptions, and actively to seek these out. This approach stems from a process called *reflective practice*. It was devised by Donald Schön, (1983, 1987).

Like Eraut, Schön was aware that professionals draw upon their tacit knowledge. Schön argued that people do think about what they do, both at the time of any activity, called 'reflecting in action', and then later, called 'reflection on action'. Reflection in action is a bit like a running commentary, in which you note what is happening as you do something and adjust accordingly. For example, you may notice people 'switching off' during a presentation, and decide to get people working in small groups to avoid them all dozing off. Reflection on action is retrospective, something you may do after the event. In this example, you may decide not to use the presentation in the same way in future, as it has not held people's attention. You therefore have 'reflected on your practice' and changed it as a result.

There are many ways to help us think reflectively. Peters (1994) provides a model that asks us to think of a concrete example and then to step back and allow ourselves to test out what are our assumptions about that situation. Brookfield (1995) suggests we can look at a situation from our own viewpoint, from our colleagues' viewpoints, from those of students, and also from perspectives derived from theoretical literature. He calls these the four critical lenses. Flanagan (1954), asks us to think of examples, perhaps with a particular characteristic, as exemplars of the phenomenon we are studying. We might want to think about sessions we have taught in which everything went well, and contrast these with sessions where things went badly wrong. These 'critical incidents' provide useful information for us to reflect upon. We can begin to uncover the characteristics about the two cases and perhaps identify trends.

Reflecting critically on our practice is not something that is achieved easily. As Hillier (2002) argues, simply reflecting on our practice does not necessarily mean that we challenge our own assumptions, or lead to change. We must be careful not to 'collude' with ideas that are comfortable for us, or rely on our colleagues to help 'bump' us into thoughts that are more challenging. However, critical reflection is a key part of practitioner research, because it enables people to ask questions about 'the way we do things around here', and creates a space for conducting research.

If we are truly reflective, we are likely to want to change what we do as a result. Deciding that we want to change something is all very well, but what change should we make, and do we know if the new version is going to be any better than the last version. Research aimed at change is something that is ongoing and active, rather than retrospective. We are not interested in analysing what has happened, but what is happening. In other words, we need to research our action, something that is called unsurprisingly action research! Let us consider an example

A course tutor's perspective

Mandy Williams teaches Care NVQs, and works with a variety of learners who are studying for a number of linked qualifications, including Nursery Nursing, Access to Nursing and Access to Social Work. Before that, she was looking after her own children. Her first job was in nursing. Mandy is on the college Board of Studies as a staff representative for her faculty of human and social sciences.

There have been numerous initiatives introduced into the college in the last few years: competence based qualifications, problem based learning, information learning technology, widening participation for under represented groups. Mandy has hardly time to get used to running her programmes according to one set of regulations when another new procedure is introduced. She feels as though she is constantly changing the way she works without having the opportunity to find out if she is being effective.

What could Mandy do to examine the way that she facilitates the learning of her different groups of people? What would help her identify what works, why she is being asked to adapt and change, how effective are these changes and what consequences follow from such changes?

Mandy is not in a position to take time off to create a large research project. She can, however, apply for a small research award from her college to examine an area of her professional practice. She has to make a case for gaining this award and design her project. Chapters 3 and 5 discuss in detail how she can do this. However, it is clear that Mandy will not have much time or many resources to undertake her research project. This is an example of a situation in which small-scale research can be conducted

Small-scale research

What do we mean by small-scale research? Imagine a situation in which the LSDA has commissioned research into teaching and learning practices that may foster retention for young people aged between 14-16. The Agency may invite colleges from across the country to participate. There may be 20 colleges, representing different types of provision, different geographical regions, and different sizes of student provision. There may be five programmes in each college that have been selected. This study will therefore be working with one hundred courses, possibly two thousand learners and a further hundred teaching staff. This is a large-scale study. Imagine a course tutor is also interested in finding out how to improve the retention of her group of 14-16 year olds. This course tutor may use a similar methodology to the large-scale study but the *scale* of her research will be much smaller. This does not mean that her study is any less valid, or important. It does mean that she cannot claim that her findings and insights gained from the research will be generalised across all further education programmes of learning. What she does gain, however, is an understanding of *her* context, *her* learners, and *her* professional practice.

Action research

Often, when people embark on small-scale research, they want to make a difference to their practice. They may be examining a new procedure, or be trying to find out if a change they have made to their resources have helped their learners more effectively. When people are researching into something that they are *doing*, with a view to making a difference as a result of their research, then they are engaged in something called *action research*. Action research does not only consist of people's reflections on what they have done. It is research while action is taking place. In other words, it is a deliberate attempt to examine the way in which something is being undertaken, with a view to making changes to that process as the research goes along. It is therefore a more fluid and iterative process than evaluation of past practice.

The 'father' of action research is Kurt Lewin (1948), who advocated that research that did not lead to any impact on improving people's lives was worthless. He worked on using research and action to change and therefore to improve aspects of people's lives such as housing, employment as well as the social context in which people live, including being recipients of, and constructors of prejudice.

An underlying philosophical principle for action research can be found in the work of Habermas (1974), who identifies that one form of knowledge, *emancipatory,* is that which not only changes people's lives but also enables them to step out of their assumptions and challenge practices which are constraining of certain groups. Action research, then, is about making a difference but doing so in a way that is informed by careful research. It requires self-reflection because we cannot possibly ensure that we want to make changes to a current situation unless we begin to think analytically about it. This is something that Dewey (1933) was keen to encourage. John Dewey, writing in the early 20th century, was a keen advocate of reflective thinking, and was influential in the American education system. Dewey argued that we should make careful observations, and then create hypotheses that we could test through action. He did not advocate rushing in on a trial and error basis.

A further feature of action research is that it is participative. In other words, it aims to enable people to improve their own practice, rather than have 'improvements' done to them. It is self-critical and is located in an approach that aims to develop practice through systematic enquiry and through learning. It is iterative in the sense that someone may start with a thought, having reflected on a particular aspect of daily practice. A systematic enquiry into that practice may ensue, perhaps with colleagues' collaboration. The results of this may lead to a change that is monitored and evaluated. Throughout this process the action may be continually refined as a result of critical reflection.

Let us consider Mandy. Mandy has been asked to work with the new Curriculum 2000. There were difficulties in the first year of its implementation, where learners in some programmes fared badly in their AS examinations and dropped out of the college. The Principal of the college has asked Mandy to work with a group of colleagues who are teaching the AS and A level syllabus in Psychology and Sociology as well as the Access to Social Work and Access to Nursing programmes. It appears that the Access programmes actually retain learners more effectively than the more 'traditional' academic A and AS level programmes. What can the staff do to improve the retention and therefore achievement rates of the learners on the A and AS level programmes?

Mandy could simply suggest a different teaching strategy and hope that her colleagues can implement it quickly. However, no one will know how well this strategy is doing until the retention figures are collected. By then, it may be too late and another group of learners will have dropped out. A further difficulty is that Mandy may not know why the Access learners stay on and successfully complete their studies. She may attribute one way of working with them, perhaps working in small groups and fostering an autonomous approach to studying psychology, to the success of the programme, when it may simply be that the learners are all mature and want to be there, compared with the A and AS level group who are much younger and are there because they did not know what else to do. How does Mandy know that her ideas will work? Can she afford to wait a year to find out?

Action research, then, is an appropriate tool to help Mandy here. Essentially, Mandy can set out, with her colleagues, to investigate some of the factors that may contribute to the different success rates of the two programmes. They may try out new teaching methods, discuss any consequences of this early on in the project and make some changes which are then also subject to enquiry and debate. The underpinning rationale for this approach is one of continual examination, checking and rechecking that ideas work, and if not, why not, and to reflect on the consequences of actions as they are taken. This process is an iterative process, in which one activity can lead to a different activity, which then is refined after further examination. It is not cyclical, in which a loop is followed around and repeated.

So action research is an approach, and has a fundamental and explicit aim to make a difference. It is inherently bound up with reflective practice, in which a group of colleagues challenge the taken for granted and try to create a rationale for their practice. Within this approach, we need to find out what works, what happens as a result, what changed. To do this, we need to apply research methods, tools which can help us answer our questions.

Finding out more

Dewey, J. (1933) *How we think: A Restatement of the Relation of Reflective Thinking in the Educative Process* Chicago: Henry Regnery

Hillier, Y. (2002) *Reflective Teaching in Further and Adult Education* London: Continuum

McNiff, J., Lomax, P., and Whitehead, J. (1996) *You and your Action Research Project* London: Routledge

Schön, D. (1983) *The Reflective Practitioner* New York: Basic Books

Schön, D. (1987) *Educating the Reflective Practitioner: Towards a New Design for Teaching and Learning in the Professions* San Francisco: Jossey Bass

Stenhouse, L. (1975) *An Introduction to Curriculum Research and Development* London: Heinemann

Chapter 5
Practical considerations in designing and conducting research

Most teachers in further education have supervised learning projects in one form or another. They know how important it is to encourage their learners to plan what they are going to do for these projects. Their learners will need to have a clear goal, an idea of what resources they need, how much time they need, with whom they should talk, where they must find sources of information and how they should present their findings. These are exactly the same as the requirements for planning research. The fundamental questions are:

- What do you want to find out and why?

- How will you do this?

- How much time will it take?

- How will you analyse the information you have acquired?

- How will you inform others?

Let us consider the main requirements of designing a research project by examining a case study. We want to know if last year's recruitment campaign was more successful in attracting young people with lower grade GCSEs. We know that this group might be encouraged to continue on to further and even higher education if they are supported in their decision of what to do next after leaving school in their sixteenth year. We also know that the local sixth forms in our college catchment area are trying to encourage their pupils to stay on into the sixth form. Can we identify if our provision is more suitable for some learners than others? What is our role in the government drive to encourage young people to keep on learning?

This situation is highly complex. We have a number of learning providers in the locality, all offering different programmes of learning, with different organisational cultures and with different approaches to recruiting learners. We may not have sufficient baseline information about the number of learners targeted from previous recruitment campaigns. We do not know why some young people choose one institution over another, or why they do not choose one at all.

This scenario presents us with numerous research goals. We might want to concentrate on finding a marketing strategy which would be aimed at particular 'niche' sections of the local population. We might want to examine our links with schools and identify if there are any effective means to facilitate the transition from school to college. We may want to identify if there are any perceived barriers to further learning within the school leavers group and how to address these. In other words, we can tackle the decision to increase the number of young people attending our college from an institutional perspective, sociological perspective or psychological perspective. We actually need to address all of these issues, but the way in which we do so will change according to our research interests and desired outcomes.

We have not yet, then, found a specific question that we wish to address. Let us start with a hypothesis, or 'hunch'. For example, we may think that the reason few young people with lower GCSE grades come to our college is that they are recruited onto job training schemes where they can gain qualifications in the workplace. Our hunch is that they think college is for people who are going into particular types of job which require qualifications, such as nursery nurses, or technicians. We think that they do not know what a further education college can offer them. If this is our hunch, then we can test our idea by finding evidence, both to support our claim but importantly to identify where our claim is not upheld. This approach of testing hypotheses is firmly rooted in a scientific approach to constructing knowledge, and Karl Popper (1972) in particular advocated that we learn more from finding what does *not* work, than from affirming what does. The difficulty with affirming what we think is the case is that we still do not know why such a situation happens. However, when we find that our evidence contradicts our ideas, then we can begin to develop new hypotheses that are more refined than our previous ideas or hunches.

Even if we do not have a clear hypothesis, we do need to have a clear idea of what we want to research. It is no good rushing into a school to talk to young people if you have not decided in advance the areas you wish to explore and why you are doing so. One way to help you clarify your ideas is to set out a proposal which answers the following questions

- What do you want to find out?

- What is the context for your question?

- Do you have any information, figures, that you can draw upon to support your question?

- Can you locate your question in a field of study? (sociology, psychology, politics)

- What are the outcomes that you hope to achieve from your research?

- How will you undertake your research? (which research approach, which methods)

- Are there different ways of answering your research question? Why have you rejected these?

- How can you justify your choice of method on the grounds of validity, accuracy and authenticity?

- What is the scope for your research? (sampling: how many people, how many centres/sites, how much staff time and other resources will this take?)

- How will you record your data?

- How will you analyse your data?

- How will you present your findings?

- What is the timescale? (what will you do when?)

- How will you be able to gain access to the people and information your require?

- How will you ensure that you are behaving in an appropriate manner? (ethical considerations, who owns the data, confidentiality, the effect you have on the people you research?)

- What will you do with the research findings? (what use will they be to 'beneficiaries')

- How will you evaluate the research process that you have used?

This list may seem daunting. However, many is the time we have watched our students enthusiastically set off to ask a set of interview questions, or send out a questionnaire and then be dumbfounded about how to analyse the results. If there is one point that anyone undertaking research should learn at the outset, it is that planning is everything! It does not matter if your research does not go according to plan, it does matter that you started out with one. It is exactly the same as lesson planning. You may find that your learners require some additional input on a topic and you realise that you will have to re-arrange your planned session half way through the lesson. This is the mark of being professional, being able to make informed decisions and alter practice in light of information and feedback. Designing research is no different in this respect. If you have anticipated as many possible factors as you can prior to setting out to undertake research, then you are more likely to gain the information you require. As John Cowan so charmingly put it, 'if you don't know where you are going, any bus will do' (Cowan, 1999)

Your research plan should contain four key components:

- Decisions about the context (orienting decisions)
- Decisions about the research design and methodology
- Decisions about the data analysis
- Decisions about presenting and reporting the findings (Cohen, Manion and Morrison, 2000)

The decisions can be represented in a decision matrix. The example in Figure 5.1 draws upon a more detailed matrix provided by Cohen, Manion and Morrison (2000).

Question	Issues and problems	Decisions
Who is the research for?	Who could use the research? Will the data be public? Can people refuse to participate?	Find out what control respondents have over the data
What is the purpose of the research?	Are there any hidden agendas? Who decides the purpose? Are there multiple purposes being served?	Determine all possible uses of the research Determine powers of respondents to control the research Identify audiences and decide on formats for reporting
What is the timescale?	Can the research be undertaken within the timescale	Decide on timing and identify plan Translate research aims into concrete questions
How can the research purposes be operationalised into methodology?	Do the research questions cover the overall research purpose? Are the questions appropriate and able to suggest ways to gather data?	Specify appropriate data types
What is the main methodology?	How many methodologies are required? Will triangulation be required?	Decide type and number of methodologies Ensure most appropriate methodologies are employed
What kinds of data are required?	Identify if numerical, words, or both required Does the research require facts or opinions or both?	Determine appropriate data for research questions Identify the balance for subjective and 'objective' data collection
How will data be gathered?	What kinds of tools and instruments will be used Will some methods be unsuitable for certain situations?	Decide on instruments Pilot instruments Identify if more than one instrument required Decide if one instrument will cover all participants
How will data be analysed?	Data processed numerically or verbally? Computer packages to be used? Statistical tests needed? Processing of open ended questions?	Decide which methods of analysis are appropriate for the types of data gathered Check the data analysis methods chosen are valid and serve the research purposes
How will the results be presented?	Who will write the report? What kind of format for different kinds of data? How will the different audiences affect the report format?	Identify the stakeholders Decide status of each report Decide timing and number of reports Devise summaries of the full report Create different types of report for different audiences

Figure 5.1: Decision matrix

There is a marked difference between having a research question, designing the research, creating a proposal (particularly if you are applying for funding or resources), and what happens in practice. Your research design is where you would set out, in an ideal world, what you want to find out and how. Your proposal may have to take account of specific research interests of the funding body, whether it is a research council, a local voluntary organisation, college funds, or for a European project. You may find that your original design has to be adapted to meet the funding requirements, or that the funds you subsequently do receive will not enable you to achieve everything you designed. Your research project, therefore, can be changed before you even begin to undertake the research.

Finally, there will be constraints that occur as the project progresses. For example, people you had hoped to interview may have left an organisation, moved away or refuse to be interviewed. The number of interviews you originally planned to do could not be done within the timescale, or within the funding given. There may have been slippage in your timescale, and the time when most people were available, or less busy has elapsed, giving you less time for interviews. You can plan for some of this by building in additional time prior to a project starting, or identifying 'back up' groups of people to interview or survey. It is a good idea to build in plenty of time for analysing data, finding resources and making contact with people. A good rule of thumb is to think of the amount of time you expect your project to take, and double it.

Below is a standard project proposal format, with questions to help you think carefully about your intended research.

1. Title

2. Background

What is the context for your research? For example, are you interested in teaching and learning methods, quality assurance, widening participation? Why are you interested in this area? Are there any recent initiatives that you are implementing that has affected your area of interest?

3. Review of literature

What has already been researched in the issue you are interested in? Are there reports of research that are relevant, even if not in your own area of investigation? Are there policy documents that are central to the issue? (see chapter 6 for more on reviewing the literature).

By the end of this review, you should have expressed the precise question that you wish to consider in your research

4. Aims and objectives

State the aim and objectives for your research. It is customary to have one main aim and a small number of objectives, five is a sensible number. Remember, the aim is your overall target for the research, and the objectives are the stepping stones to help you get there. This is exactly the way that you would construct learning aims and objectives (see Hillier, 2002).

5. Outcomes

List what you hope to have achieved as a result of the project. This could be a new resource, a set of recommendations, a new policy or an analytical account of a phenomenon you are investigating.

6. Method

What is your overall approach? Are you going to use existing evidence and examine it? Are you going to repeat an earlier research but in a different context? Do you anticipate using numerical data, or qualitative data, or both? Try to start with the overall research approach, then discuss your methods and how you intend to analyse the data. State the scale of the project, for example, how many interviews will you conduct, how many questionnaires will you distribute, what is the size of your sample?

7. Timescale

Provide a plan for each stage of the research. Remember, some activities will occur concurrently. Others cannot take place until you have completed an earlier phase. Remember to allow time for a pilot of your research tool, and time for setting up any interviews, devising questionnaires and gaining data sets.

8. Access

State how you will gain access to the people and information you are seeking. Do you need a letter of support from your supervisor or manager? Will you be working with minors, and if so, do you need to go through security checks? (Remember, this will take time, so include this in your timescale plan, too)

9. Ethical considerations

What particular issues arise from your research design regarding ethical considerations? For example, how will you deal with confidentiality? What is your role in the research compared with your relationship with the people you intend to conduct the research on? Who owns the data?

10 Resources required

What do you need to conduct your research? This includes your own time, use of photocopier, access to the internet, telephone, postage. Do not underestimate the resources you will need to conduct your research.

11. Dissemination of findings

How will you write up and report your results? Who is the research for and what is the audience for your report? Will there be different reports for different audiences? If you are undertaking a research project for a postgraduate qualification, you will have different criteria than that for a management report in your college. Can you manage to balance the requirements of both?

12. Future research

Can you anticipate additional research that could follow on from your proposed small-scale research?

Gaining Access

We cannot presume that we have permission to seek information from people and data sources just because we work within the FE sector. People increasingly are covered by legislation such as the Data Protection Act, so that their personal information is not given out to other individuals without their consent. This has far reaching consequences for the way in which we conduct research. Supposing

I want to talk to a group of trainees who completed a New Deal project last year in the music industry. They were young, black males who, being unemployed, were encouraged to further their education. The New Deal project was aimed at enabling them to find work within the cultural industries, a particularly expanding area within the UK. It would make sense for me to find out where they live and arrange to talk to them, either by telephone or in person. I do not have permission to gain access to their addresses, even though they have been trainees at an organisation which runs NVQs as a satellite centre of my college. If I do obtain their addresses and make contact with them, I am breaking the law.

It is understandable that researchers want to visit people in organisations, work places and learning centres, particularly if their research is asking questions about the learning process, or how people are engaged with meeting their personal learning goals. On the other hand, there have to be safeguards against intruders, people acting unprofessionally, and a general protocol to ensure security and safety for all individuals within an organisation, in this case staff and learners.

There are ways to obtain permission and gain access to undertake your research. The first step is to identify who you should contact to gain official permission to conduct your research. It is worth contacting the organisation by telephone, or searching the website before you write your letter, to ensure that you have identified the most appropriate person from whom you can seek permission.

State clearly what your research is about and why you are doing it. If you are working towards a qualification such as a diploma or masters degree, then state this in your letter. If you have funding from a particular funding body, then make sure you include this information. Remember that your research may yield important and helpful information for the organisation concerned and you should state this in your letter. Try to identify what commitment is required from the individuals you wish to speak with and, if you are able at this stage, to specify how many people will be involved. It helps if you can specify the timescale but this is something which is usually negotiated once you have gained permission. For example, you may wish to interview heads of department in three further education colleges. There may be particular institutional demands on one college such as preparing for inspection that will mean that you will have to delay your research there for a few weeks. It is important to establish a good, open relationship with the people you will be dealing with. If you are clear about what you wish to achieve but are flexible to fit in with institutional and personal constraints, then you will be giving positive signals about your approach to the research, and you will be more likely to succeed in gaining access to the organisation and the people who work there.

You may find it helpful to write a short summary of the research project which can be disseminated to potential participants. You could anticipate questions they may ask, and write a short statement about what their involvement would be. You should also write a statement about anonymity and confidentiality, whether participants will see draft reports, what will be done with information they provide and how this will be presented or placed in the public domain.

The context

What do we mean by context? One way is to think of the meaning of a situation. We often work out an unknown word in a passage by taking account of the context. When we talk about context for research purposes, we are referring to the situation and its meaning for us. For example, we may want to look at student retention in our college. Now the context for this could be to do with funding, to do with achievement, or to do with a new management information system. So the context helps define the kind of questions we wish to ask. People often limit their research questions to a very narrow contextual base and it is important to try and define the context as widely as possible in the initial stages, before focussing on a particular aspect. One helpful way to do this is to think of your project idea and try to identify which fields of study it relates to.

Now you have outlined your context, you can begin to focus on what you want to find out. It is almost impossible to undertake research which covers all the areas you will have identified in your diagram.

The single most important decision to make with a research design is by which approach and methods the research question can be tackled. Once we have chosen one approach over the other, we can

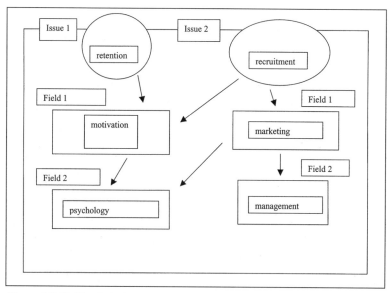

Figure 5.2: Fields of study

then decide exactly how many people are involved, what sources of information and how long we have to gather this information. If you are writing a research proposal for a project as part of a postgraduate award, or for a funding body, you will have to justify your research methodology. As you will see in later chapters, there are enormous variations in the way you can conduct research. At this stage in your research planning, you need to consider carefully which approach is suitable. One way to do this is to identify all the pros and cons of different approaches in relation to your research question. There is always a compromise with research approaches and methods. If you decide to survey large numbers of people, you may not gain depth from the information you receive. If you decide to concentrate on a small group or single case, you will not be able to extrapolate to the wider population. If you ask for people's perceptions, you may not capture more publicly available 'facts'. If you rely on desk-based research from publications and sources in the public domain, you will not have the 'human' angle. Your decision, ultimately, stands or falls by how you justify it. There is endless debate within educational research circles about what counts as research, and how it should be conducted. You have to be bold and make decisions, knowing that your approach will not yield the full picture. Doing nothing is not a tenable position!

It can be daunting to read educational research text books. Much educational research focuses on school and compulsory education, with little relevance to the vast and complex work undertaken in further education and the learning and skills sector.

Our view is that research is a dynamic process. Thirty years ago, working with single case studies was almost unheard of. Teachers subsequently began to be encouraged to become researchers (see Stenhouse, 1975, Simons, 1980, Elliot, 1991). Yet these approaches have become more mainstream over time. This is precisely where the further education research agenda is today. Our approach will clearly draw upon good practice in other educational areas but there is something distinctive about the FE sector that will interact with the way we ask research questions, conduct research, disseminate our findings and implement action on the basis of these.

Finding out more

Bell, J. (1993) *Doing your Research Project* (2nd edn) Buckingham: Open University Press

Cohen, L., Manion, L., and Morrison, K. (2000) *Research methods in Education* (5th edn) London: Routledge

Denscome, M. (2002) *Ground Rules for Good Research: a 10 point guide for social researchers* Buckingham: Open University Press

Orna, E. and Stevens, J. (1995) *Managing Information for Research* Buckingham: Open University Press

Chapter 6
Finding information and literature reviews

Marco is trying to locate information sources for his PhD thesis, which he is carrying out in a local university, on top of his main work as a business studies lecturer in further education. He has decided that his research question is: *'How effectively are local further education and training providers identifying and meeting the training needs of businesses in Researchborough?'* Marco is knowledgeable about the geographical area and the needs of local businesses, having lived and worked in Researchborough for a number of years. He is also generally familiar with the use of computer and library resources, but finds it hard to distinguish between the many results he gets when he carries out an information search.

Having decided and agreed with his university supervisor the main topic for his thesis, Marco is finding it difficult to move beyond the initial stages of information searching. He is keen on exploring relevant fields of knowledge and information, but needs some guidance. Here are some things that would be useful for Marco to consider.

Developing an information search strategy and tailoring this to original research

- define the research question clearly

- target useful sources of information, including web-based

- acknowledge strengths and weaknesses in your research starting point

- plan and manage the information strategy

- carry out a background search on ideas and hunches

- link information sources to your own ideas

- be selective about what to include

- concentrate on using relevant background material

- develop a strategy for analysing information

- cite sources properly – using protocol and formats

Define the research question clearly

First, Marco needs to identify his reasons for gathering information. Clearly, this means focusing his PhD topic into a series of main themes. He will need to undertake a wide-ranging study of the research literature available in these areas that goes beyond initial searching for background information. Having identified and read a wide range of publications in areas directly related to his research thesis, Marcus then needs to probe deeply into these sources, distinguishing between them in terms of quality, relevance and currency.

Marco will need to select out the work of expert opinion leaders in the research field, identify contentious and problematic areas, and gaps in existing research and knowledge. Having widely surveyed and evaluated the thematic fields of study in his area, Marco then needs to focus down into areas that interest him the most and, within these areas, to develop his own thesis. This thesis is not just the paper document he will produce for the PhD, but consists of the ideas and arguments that are his own, and that will form his original contribution to knowledge in this area.

Target useful information sources, including web-based information

Marco needs to select from amongst the following sources those most appropriate to his information and overall research needs. Here are some of the resources available to him:

People:
- university and FE research groups and key informants, librarians, expert academic staff fellow students

- colleagues at work and in local groups

- information personnel in governmental agencies and associations

Books and other publications:

- local and national newspapers

- local journals, leaflets, guidebooks, other 'grey' literature

- reference books and other resources in university and public libraries

- previous research journal articles and reports on the subject

- research papers listed in citation indexes and government databases

Internet and other information technology resources:

- web search engines and meta-search engines

- websites specialising relating to the topics in question

- citation indexes, government databases, and other 'grey literature'

- e-journals, e-books, e-zines (magazines on the internet), CDRoms

- newsgroups and bulletin boards

Events and places:

- university library, public library, specialist libraries

- public and private collections in museums and galleries

- governmental agencies and groups

Television, radio, video and other media:

- television and radio programmes

- rental, public and private VHS and DVD programmes

Of all of these many sources, valuable information provided by knowledgeable people, relevant journal articles and books, and web-based information sources, perhaps provide the most significant initial areas to target. Web-based search engines such as *google.com* or *teoma.com* are particularly useful for a very quick identification of key issues and sources potentially available, from which searches can be further developed.

Marco may already have compiled an extensive bibliography for previous work, and used different methods for information retrieval. He may have found he could not find some relevant information sources, and felt swamped by the amount of data he found. He may have found it difficult to analyse the level of importance of the information he found. Marco will have unique experience and qualities of his own as a researcher, and perhaps some areas that need improvement.

For example, if he knows he is a person who always wants to read every available information source and doesn't tend to leave enough time for writing, he could help himself by arranging a series of submission deadlines with his supervisor that will require him to limit the time for information searching. Alternatively, if he knows that he is a good planner, methodical and timely about writing, but tends to lack imagination, he could plan to spend some time 'brainstorming' his topic with a research group to develop his ideas.

Sometimes people with long-standing connections in an area of study or with good local knowledge can save a huge amount of time by helping students quickly cut through the navigation of what seems initially to be impenetrable territory. There is often no real substitute for *expert advice* and opinion, particularly in a face-to-face meeting. This may be particularly useful to help focus the area of study, and cut down the need to investigate fruitless sources.

Learn to plan and manage an information search strategy

Marco therefore needs to *plan* and *manage* his strategy for information search and evaluation. Literature search is an area in which people often get lost, overwhelmed by the vast amount of information available. It is also an area which is expanding enormously, because of internet web-based facilities.

The huge amount of information now available on the web means that the skills of seeking out, retrieving and using information effectively are key areas to develop. Anyone can put information into a computer, but to locate appropriate sources of information and use these effectively for developing relevant, useful, applicable expert knowledge is a highly advanced skill – that of the 'knowledge worker'.

Carry out a background search on ideas and hunches

Often research starts with an idea, or series of hunches about a particular area – and then researchers carry out work to see if their hunches can be affirmed or discounted. The 'hunch' is essentially an informed intuitive guess often made by a practitioner, working from their own 'tactic knowledge' of the field to be researched.

Practitioners possess advanced understanding that has come from many years of experience. This understanding may be informing their ideas at a background level, but perhaps initially they may find it difficult to verbalise the reasons for the 'hunch' or to frame their ideas into the structured form of a research proposal.

Remember a researcher needs to have an overall imaginative conceptualisation of the basic idea behind the research, before any work can actually be carried out. Marco needs to visualise and articulate his 'hunch' before he can go anywhere with his ideas. The use of imaginative metaphors, models and brainstorming methods to tease out the key factors involved in a hunch are useful techniques, remember Newton's imaginative use of the apple to formulate a theory of gravity!

An important part of the process of researching vague 'hunches' is therefore to undertake a brainstorming exercise using an initial literature search to test out the practical workability of an idea. Sometimes, the issue Marco is about to research might be very topical and recently written about in newspapers and reports, mentioned on television and discussed by his colleagues. However, in some cases, the topics of key interest will not have been written about very much.

Having realistically evaluated his starting point and brainstormed the general area, Marco may decide he is interested in finding out more about a series of particular issues or topics within it. He may not know much about these, but perhaps has a rough idea that it would be useful to investigate, for example, the quantity and range of small and medium enterprises in the area in Researchborough, how many people are employed in them, and how much training they do, in which sectoral areas. One of the important things he then must do is to find out what has already been found out on this kind of topic.

Identify gaps in research and make a case for own new ideas

The aim of this kind of literature search for Marco would be to justify *his own* approach to the topic, demonstrate that the research will add something to his knowledge and professional practice, perhaps by testing out someone else's ideas in a new context or replicating a study with a different group of learners.

Find out about methods and processes used in previous relevant research

Marco can also find out *how* people have researched his topic. It is important that he does not start his own research without having at least tried to see what other people have done about the topic he's interested in. They may have developed unusual methods of inquiry, based on the needs of the subject area. He may find that he does not agree with their approach and wants to try a different way to find out the information he's interested in. If he does not undertake a literature search, there is a danger he may use an inappropriate methodology, repeat mistakes others have made and this may culminate in wasting time.

Be selective

Marco does not necessarily need to spend hours on an exhaustive search of everything written about his topic. If his topic is an extensively-researched area, this may also be neither practical nor possible.

Make a background case for research based on the literature

Deciding to carry out research is one thing, but providing a coherent case for the research question to be undertaken is another. Marco needs to consider the following:

- making a background case for his research

- the nature and range of his information sources

- how many to use: what scope, what limits

- difficulties he might encounter when searching for information

- difficulties of access to some information sources

- few references for his topic

- materials that are out of print or unobtainable

- obscure references

- instability of website sources of information

If Marco has been following a particular issue for some time, he may already have read some of the literature, or be aware of some key texts already. If he is starting from scratch, then an important way in is to undertake a search of internet and library sources using key words. Marco could make a note of how many references he obtains for his subject. It will help to be very specific about his search, as in the example provided above. Sometimes researchers can spend considerable time vaguely exploring the general literature before being able to decide exactly what it is they wish to pursue. They can get interested in the general issues and wander about, failing to focus for too long.

An additional problem is that if researchers are not clear about specifying exactly what they want to explore, they can't be sure they're looking in the right place for the information needed. So it helps to have a clear specification of the research question as soon as this is feasible. This need not be a final title for the research, and it may be amended as the research develops, but it does help the researcher begin to focus. It's a bit like jumping in the deep end and forcing yourself to swim.

Marco will need to think about the date of the information sources, as recent references are often very useful. They often contain references to earlier, definitive work and provide up to date analyses of the context, something particularly important for the rapidly changing world of further education.

Since further education colleges also often have links to local businesses, Marco could also directly access their prospectuses or websites, but he will again need to be selective about the range and quality of information.

Specialist research databases

Neither free web-based search engines nor more limited library catalogues will necessarily contain all the appropriate and useful information that will ultimately meet Marco's requirements. There are, however, a number of specialist research databases he could find particularly useful.

These databases contain information about books, and also articles and reports on specific areas. Some will also provide not just the abstract of the article but the full text. Gaining access to these databases is restricted. Many require you to be a student or member of staff in a higher education institution, or at least to pay as a subscriber. An example of one of these databases, which is for educational research, is the Bath Information Database Service (BIDS) database. There are also on-line journal articles, newsgroups and discussion forums.

Web-based search and metasearch engines

Google (http://www.google.com) is the biggest search engine database in the world, and claims to have over three billion pages. It is also different from some other search engines because of its *ranking algorithm*. This is based on how many other pages link to each page. Other factors are also included in the search, such as the proximity of search keywords or phrases in documents.

Google also lets you do a full text search of *.pdf* Acrobat files on the web, which no other search engine yet does. You can do simple or advanced searches, image searches, easy searches using OR (for example, WOMAN OR WOMEN), phrase searching (for example, 'American wars'), exclusion searches (for example, excluding a term by putting a hyphen in front of it as a minus sign, such as you could use in 'American wars – Vietnam).

To come up with results to a search, Google uses not only the number of other pages that link to a page, but also the importance of the links. This is measured by the links that there are to each of these links in turn. No-one is able to buy or influence the ranking of pages in Google, unlike some other search engines, which also gives Google an authenticity based on objective evidence.

Other very useful search engines are as follows below.

*   http://www.alltheweb.com
*   http://www.teoma.com
*   http://www.altavista.com
*   http://www.surfwax.com
*   http://www.copernic.com

Almost none of the free meta-search engines allow you to search fully through Google, which is ranked by many as the best search information database in the world. Therefore, it's often best to just try Google first, and then move on to meta-search engines if you have not found what you are looking for and want to try other sources.

It's useful to consider how professional researchers and journalists find information, and the mechanisms that are there to help like meta-search engines, citation indexes. These can assist someone like Marco to work out what was missing from the literature that he had, and find out how to go about plugging any gaps?

The 'invisible' or 'deep' web

The 'invisible' or 'deep' web consists of documents existing at deeper layers than are immediately available as web pages searchable by ordinary search engines. The information is therefore 'invisible' to search engines, for example content-rich database information that exists in university, government and company databases. Specific software can be purchased to search through the invisible web, called Lexibot, available from *BrightPlanet.com.*

Undertaking a web search

Marco may have been pondering what he could do to find out about all the training needs of local businesses in Researchborough. He wants to know what has been done recently, what the definitive works are and perhaps something about his own particular context.

From an initial web-search on *google.com*, Marco finds out that there are many sources of information about 'local businesses in Researchborough', but a much smaller number of these also contain information relating to 'further education'. Of these, there are fewer still that also have references relating to 'training needs' and 'colleges'. Marco might therefore want to focus initially on only the first 20 or so sources, of which perhaps several may contain repeated information. Refining his focus on these still further, he may find that there are just five really useful key articles about his topic, that within themselves contain more specialist references to better quality printed journal and book articles in the field. Marco follows these items up. He is now beginning to be usefully selective with both his research focus and use of time (see example below).

If Marco types in

local businesses Researchborough<

he will end up with a very large number of references of around 160,000.

However, if he types in

local businesses Researchborough further education training needs colleges<

he will narrow the number of references down considerably to around 6,000.

He will not yet know which references are worth pursuing, but since most web search engines will rank the links according to relevance, he could now pursue the first 20 or so links he is given, and follow through by printing these, reading them and pursuing the further links within them.

Figure 6.1 Web search example

The amount of literature Marco needs to study will depend on why he is doing the research in the first place, the number of information sources available, if there are particular requirements he has to meet and importantly, how much time he has to spend. If Marco spends all his available time reading about local businesses and training, he may never get around to doing any research of his own! This is why it is critically important to be selective with information sources, and use expert advice to cut through unnecessary fruitless material.

Citation indexes

Citation indexes are multidisciplinary indexes of bibliographic information drawn from thousands of research journals, that track references authors have put in the bibliographies of published articles. These indexes give us a way to search for and analyse literature in a way not possible through simple keyword/topical searching.

The use of citation indexes is controlled by the *Institute for Scientific Information*, the publisher of the three main citation indexes available today:

- Science Citation Index (SCI),

- Social Sciences Citation Index (SSCI), and

- Arts and Humanities Citation Index (AHCI).

Citation indexing allows the researcher to look 'forward' in the literature, from the starting point of a particular article or group of articles. This is a different method that complements literature searching.

Bibliographic referencing

Recognising other writers' work and showing sources on which your work is based is important. This standard practice also enables other researchers follow up your information leads and obtain further information for themselves from these in turn. You need to record references accurately when drawing up your bibliography, using a standard system such as the Harvard referencing system.

Harvard system

The Harvard system of citation was developed in the USA and has become the most popular system internationally, being used as the standard house style for many academic journals. It is a flexible and straightforward system, clear and useful for both authors and readers, because all that is needed in the text of the work is to mention of the author and date of publication [for example, the work of Jones (1993)], and then to list the full reference in the bibliography. This full reference allows a reader easily to find the full description of the item you have cited. It also shows instantly how up to date the reference work is, and indicates through the name of the author whether it is a well-known expert in the field. (for further information use an authoritative guide such as the Library Services at Leeds Metropolitan University at: http://www.lmu.ac.uk/lss/ls/docs/harv.htm)

Terms used for referencing:

'Bibliography' lists the information sources that you've used in your text, while a 'reference' describes in detail the item from which you obtained information, and 'citing' or 'quoting' recognises the sources of information in your text.

Keep reference notes for your bibliography

A straightforward but important technique for Marco to remember when developing his research is to keep notes and page references for all works consulted. This can save a lot of time and trouble when compiling the final bibliography. There is nothing worse than hunting through a book to try to find the page references for the sentences that you read and quoted some months ago!

Finding out more:

Chisholm, M. (2001) *The Internet Guide for Writers* Oxford: How to Books Ltd.

Hart, C. (2001) *Doing a Literature Search: A comprehensive guide for the social sciences* Buckingham: Open University Press

Wilkinson, D. (2000) *The Researcher's Toolkit: The Complete Guide to Practitioner Research* London: RoutledgeFalmer.

Chapter 7
Ethical considerations

The ethics of carrying out research is perhaps the most tricky and sensitive area of all those covered by this book. Derived from the Greek *ēthika*, the word '*ethic(s)*' means:

> The science of morals; the department of study concerned with the principles of human duty. *Oxford English Dictionary*

Applied to educational research, ethics encompasses those principles and standards of good conduct researchers should observe to ensure that research is morally justifiable, reasonable, beneficial to educational purposes, is carried out well and causes no harm to anyone or anything. In applying ethics, researchers particularly need to apply their *own judgement* in interpreting the codes of practice and general considerations on ethics that we discuss below. Researchers also need to regard each research case as unique, because the individual circumstances affecting it are different from any other.

Why consider ethics?

Why should we bother with ethics? Research ethics is a complex, well-established field, based on fundamental principles of human rights, justice and well-being for all involved in research. Its history is derived from painful lessons learned about the need to avoid negatively affecting or abusing human and animal subjects in any way. We also need to ensure that there is protection for individuals in our research practice, that everyone knows this, and that the ethical principles we follow are appropriate to the circumstances of the research. An important way to establish public confidence when carrying out research in further education institutions is to ensure we are abiding by a well-established, publicly shared *code of ethics*.

Specialist areas of ethics

Since all educational endeavour inevitably involves a range of human participants, there are diverse aspects to consider before selecting our research methods of data collection, analysis and dissemination. Specialist areas of ethics exist for each discipline-related educational research field. When carrying out research in health education, for example, we may need to consider research principles linked with medical ethics. Research work carried out on e-learning and on-line educational computing will need to encompass particular issues relating to the ethics of using the world wide web, such as copyright, plagiarism, safety and security.

Ethics is a potential minefield of different, sometimes competing views about what various schools of thought regard as 'right' or 'wrong' about different research methods and processes available for use. Ethical principles are also subject to continuously changing refinements in principles and standards, including developments in standards and codes of practice.

Being up to date

We need to be sure we are up to date in both the principles and practices in the subject area to be researched. An historical example of refinement in ethical standards might be taken from the field of psychological research. Humans who took part in psychological research were previously called 'subjects' but are now routinely called 'participants'. This significant evolution in terminology designated a profoundly important shift towards greater sensitivity and equality in the relationship between the 'researcher' and the 'researched'. Scientists carrying out experimental psychological research became increasingly sensitive to the fact that their 'subjects' are not just inert objects to be manipulated at the researcher's will, but are fully autonomous, sensate human beings needing to be recognised as such in both the terminology and procedures for carrying out research.

Other examples relate to increased awareness and sensitivity about the ways in which gender, ethnicity, culture, age, sexual preference, religion, politics and economics affect our perceptions and shapes common language usage. There are shifts in understanding about the purposes and values of research versus the 'costs' of it. Milgram's (1963, 1964) experiments in the 1960s resulted in valuable and shocking psychological understandings about the potential willingness of human participants to administer or allow the administration of shock treatments to others that would normally be seriously against their better judgement. Such research would today be regarded as unethical and would no longer be carried out. The recognition that research should not cause participants any harm is now more widely understood and practised. A cost/benefit analysis of carrying out research sometimes needs to be brought to bear in decisions relating to difficult ethical matters. This principle describes whether the 'cost' of doing the research is higher than the 'benefit' to be obtained by it, and is discussed in further detail by Cohen, Manion and Morrison (2000).

Good practice guidelines for educational research ethics have been developed by a number of organisations. These include the British Educational Research Association (BERA), the National Foundation for Education Research (NFER), the Social Research Association (SRA), the Department for Education and Skills (DfES), the Qualifications and Curriculum Authority (QCA) and others. These codes of practice generally include guidelines relating to the following areas:

- Informed consent
- Respect for participants
- Consequences of participation
- Confidentiality, privacy and anonymity
- Sensitivity to power relations
- Consideration of ownership issues
- Professionalism
- Truth
- Relativism
- Use of control groups
- Carrying out observations

Informed consent

The principle of informed consent is one of the most important areas to consider when carrying out research. With most research approaches, you must ask your participants for their consent in undertaking the research. They will need to know what it is you are trying to find out and why, how the data will be collected, what their role will be, who owns the data and what will happen to the findings. Once they have this information, they will be able to make a decision about whether or not to participate. If they do decide to participate, then they will give informed consent, in other words they will know what is going to happen and agree to it. In giving such consent, participants also need to know that they have a right not to participate, or to withdraw from participation at any time. They need to know what the consequences are of participation, non-participation and withdrawal. The risks or benefits of participation, where to go for further information, and the guidelines relating to confidentiality need to be explained to participants.

In medical research, participants' consent may not be fully informed, because the participants may not know whether they are receiving a new drug, or a placebo, a 'non-drug' that is used as a control. They should know, however, that they will receive one or the other, and that they can be given alternative treatment if they wish. In cases like this, and also in psychological research, it may be important to hold 'de-briefing' sessions after the research is complete, to ensure that participants understand the nature of the process that has occurred and are not negatively affected by it.

In ethnographic research studies, where observations are undertaken by researchers who may need to behave in the same way as the group of people they are researching, such as 'undercover' police, consent may not be able to be obtained. However, ethical principles still need to be followed relating to all other areas, including especially confidentiality, privacy and anonymity. In research carried out with some areas of educational special needs or with young children, informed consent may need to be obtained both from appropriate guardians of participants, as well as from participants themselves to the fullest extent possible. This may mean adapting briefing information to fit participants' abilities to understand what will happen in the research process. The guiding principle is to expect that we will need to ask for consent, having explained the purpose of our research. We will also need to explain to participants why we are doing the research and in what ways we will give further opportunities for potential participants to clarify any queries they may have. On page 88 we have given an example consent form for interviews from the Changing Faces project, which is examining the development of adult basic education practices from 1970-2000 (see http://lancs.ac.uk/edres/changingfaces/). The project will be offering material and interview data for future researchers, requiring a more detailed consent form for respondents to complete.

Respect for participants

We may not agree with the viewpoints of the people we interview, or from whom we obtain questionnaire responses. We may not like the way our research is providing evidence about any question we have asked. However, we must acknowledge that this is what our particular research methodology is showing us. We have to consider the issue of bias, and how we may interpret someone's responses, or the data that we have before us.

We have to acknowledge that when we undertake research we are in a situation in which we are interacting with people, either face to face, or with the outcomes of research methods in which we have asked them to participate by telling us their ideas, views, or even allowing us to observe them. We must be careful not to dismiss one person's ideas because they contradict another's. For example, it would be easy to be persuaded by views of colleagues with whom we share an enormous amount of understanding and practice, rather than by the views of a group of people with whom we have not interacted before. We are not suggesting that we deliberately set out to ignore some groups of people, but we are often unaware of how much we tend to privilege one perspective over another.

Respect for the people we are asking to participate in our research extends beyond accepting what they say. We must understand that they are giving us their time, at least, if they agree to respond to our research. Our code of practice includes ensuring that we minimise disruption, compensate for any inconvenience and thank them for their participation.

Changing Faces of Adult Literacy, Numeracy & ESOL

A Critical History of Policy and Practice 1970-2000

The project will track policy initiatives stemming from the 1970s adult literacy campaign up to the launch last year of a new adult basic skills campaign as part of the National Literacy Strategy.

CONSENT FORM

Thank you for agreeing to take part in the Changing Faces project. After the interview takes place the tape will be transcribed and a copy will be returned to you. There are several ways in which the tape and transcription may be stored and used. We would like to ask your permission about this and check that you know what your options are. Please circle all that apply.

- I have been informed about the Changing Faces project   YES/NO

- I am happy for the tape of my interview to be stored in the project's archive at Lancaster University/City University   YES/NO

- I am happy for other researchers to have access to my tape
                                                                 YES/NO

- Would you like your name to be used on the transcript?   YES/NO

- If NO please indicate a name that we may use _____

- Are you happy for the transcript to be stored by the Changing Faces Project team at Lancaster University/City University?
                                                                 YES/NO

- I do not want anyone beside the project team to see it   YES/NO

- I am happy for it to go in the archive for other researchers to see it
                                                                 YES/NO

- I am happy to have my words used:
  - a) on the project web site anonymously   YES/NO
  - b) on the project web site with my name   YES/NO
  - c) in publications anonymously   YES/NO
  - d) in publications with my name on it   YES/NO

Signed: _____Date: _____

Figure 7.1: Consent Form

Consequences of participation

Taking part in research can affect respondents in a variety of ways. They may have been asked to participate in a focus group, and find that the experience has been rewarding. Their views have been solicited and someone finally has been interested in what they have to say. Participants may be spurred on to further action as a result of doing so. On the other hand, participants may have a negative experience of participating in research. Recently, learners have been asked to participate in a pilot of the national basic skills tests. Many of the participants will have had experiences of failing tests in the past. If they fail (any many did fail) the pilot tests, then their participation is likely to reinforce their low self-esteem. What can researchers do to ensure we take steps to deal with such outcomes? We are not suggesting that researchers should be trained in counselling, or should expect people to require therapy after participating in their research. However we do suggest that researchers need to think very carefully about what may happen in their research and to have strategies for dealing with this. Will there be an opportunity for participants to talk about their experiences together, or individually with the researcher afterwards? Are there positive steps that can be taken, such as holding debriefing sessions, or giving information about further learning opportunities and using educational and careers guidance facilities? If there are problems identified from previous research, a useful question to ask is whether in future such situations can be handled in a different way, so that learners are not negatively affected.

Confidentiality, privacy and anonymity

We need to ensure appropriate standards of confidentiality, privacy and anonymity apply in our research projects. The process also needs to be conveyed to participants, so they are aware they will not be harmed in any way by participating in the research. Ensuring individual participants' anonymity in the research project, and that rights of privacy and confidentiality are respected is a key feature.

Applying standards of confidentiality and privacy is not always straightforward. Anonymity of participants can generally be achieved through the use of pseudonyms, or a numbering and coding system. However, if well-known roles within an organisation can be identified in the research, for example, if there is only one head of the sports department, it may be important to ensure people's identities are protected by changes of designation to more general ones, such as 'head of specialist area'. Some things we find out in the course of doing research may be best left undisclosed. This is particularly the case if we have been directly informed that specific items of data are confidential, but it also applies to more general principles of confidentiality applicable under the Data Protection Act (1998).

Standards and principles of confidentiality apply in different ways according to the specialist areas involved in our research. For example, research on student bullying in the college canteen may require a stricter set of protocols around confidentiality than research about whether a new car park will benefit students. In the first case, in particular, we need to consider whether the audience of the research could identify who the participants are. A research project may collect and anonymously report the views of thousands of students. We might assume that individual people's views will always be confidential in such cases, as the results will only be reported in numerical terms. But if our project singles out students with disabilities as a category in which we report responses, and if there are only a small number of such students with identifiable disabilities, it may be possible in some instances for an audience to work out the views of individual respondents by a process of elimination. Such a situation must be avoided, as it may cause embarrassment and difficulty to participants.

The eight principles of good practice relating to the Data Protection Act (1998) on the confidentiality of individual data and the rights of subject access to individual data should be observed in all research. When following these guidelines, we should make appropriate arrangements for adequate security if we hold and disseminate data about individual participants This includes being aware of the potential limitations of security in web-based and email transactions.

Sensitivity to power relations
Unequal power relations exist in all research settings. We live and interact with each other constantly in a more or less overt acknowledgement of human power relations. Power relations affecting FE

research includes: the power of *status* in terms of hierarchical institutional structures and positions of authority in FE, the power of *expertise* relating to differing levels of experience, skills and knowledge in the specialist research area; the power of *influence*, in terms of popular local opinions or moral and cultural issues raised by participants about the area to be researched; the power of *personality*, in which individuals may hold personal social power in the research process relating to their own histories, and *communicative* power; in which some participants may hold more power than others to shape the research because their views about the project are better communicated. All these kinds of power, and more, may constantly interact as the research proceeds to form the ongoing human power dynamic in the project.

These kinds of issues affect us professionally every day when working in education. When we act as tutors, teachers and managers, we have considerable power that affects our colleagues and learners. Similarly, others may have power over us. The dynamics of power are complex and subtle. They are sometimes easier to analyse definitively when we know the final results of actions, than when we are in the midst of constantly changing interactional relations. Power relations shift and develop all the time in terms of local politics affecting the research group, just as in human affairs, governments and leaders rise and fall.

For example, when planning interviews or questionnaires, we should be aware that when people talk to each other or fill in questionnaires, they often take account of the power relationship before they decide how much to disclose. It is highly unlikely that a college principal will disclose his or her feelings of insecurity before a colleague who is on a much lower grade. It is also unlikely people filling in a questionnaire will disclose information that might be damaging to them. Yet research questions may require such disclosure to provide a more accurate account of the issue being investigated.

Consideration of ownership issues

When we provide information to another person, who 'owns' that information? If I tell a colleague about a new method I have tried in my class to engage my learners in a particular topic, and my colleague writes about this in a college newsletter without acknowledging that I told her, I may feel aggrieved. I may feel that I did not give permission for my information to be disseminated. Of course, I may be pleased that my ideas are thought worthy of sharing with a wider audience, but the fact remains that I may feel my intellectual property has been displayed without my permission. I do, however, also need to examine my own sensitivities on this issue. Perhaps there have been group discussions on the research project that have led my colleague to assume that I have given 'tacit' permission for the data to be published. In such a case, my colleague would be best to ensure in advance that there is an agreement about ownership issues, and that this is tackled directly and openly as part of the planning for the research and its dissemination.

Ownership of data and authorship in research can be sensitive issues, and we should ensure we obtain appropriate, openly shared and negotiated permissions from participants and institutions involved in research to use the data we collect. At the same time, however, we should try to encourage individuals not to put intrusive blocks on the accurate and responsible portrayal of information if this is ethically and sensitively disseminated in the interests of public benefit. Sometimes people may be worried about disseminating research results containing any information that could be interpreted negatively. This type of issue around ownership is perhaps best discussed collectively by an *action research group* or similar gathering of informed interested parties and practitioners who can together arrive at a consensus on the *cost/benefit analysis* (Cohen *et al.*, 2000) involved in the research practice and dissemination.

Responsibly handling the question of ownership is therefore sometimes a question of striving to find the right balance amongst a number of parties involved in a research project. Ultimately, educational research has as its core value the principle of benefit to learners and to society in the interests of common public good. In cases needing decision between competing interests of ownership and the representation of opinions on data, therefore, once basic permissions have been sought and obtained, questions of ownershipmay perhaps be fairly resolved by considering in what ways the principle of benefit to learners is being observed in taking a particular decision.

Professionalism

Even though we may be carrying out a small-scale research project with limited resources, little time and support, and few opportunities for dissemination, we still need to ensure overall that our research is carried out in a professional way. Supervisors, research advisers and support groups can help us achieve levels of appropriate rigour, quality, consistency, insight and usefulness so that we can be proud of our work. Research is a field of endeavour in which worthwhile, unique contributions can be made by small-scale researchers working with few resources. This is particularly the case in further education, in which a number of talented researchers have already carried out ground-breaking studies that have achieved national and regional recognition. However there is room for significant new growth. Such growth needs to be achieved in ways that adhere to good quality practices.

Truth

When carrying out research, we often ask people to provide us with their viewpoints, information and to give up their time to do so. We then make sense of what they tell us through analysis of our findings. Following this, we offer evidence, based on people's words, perceptions and feelings, to our research audience. This audience often contains decision makers, who take action based on our reported findings. The opportunity for misrepresentation of people's views, and for bias in our analysis and reporting is immense. This is not to say that all researchers ignore what they find out and wilfully skew their findings. Yet the experience of, for example, taking part in committee meetings enables us to recognise that there may be as many views about a meeting as there were individuals attending it. Such understanding helps us to realise how difficult it is to have an accurate picture of any situation, and to ensure that our research report accurately reflects the complexity of different perspectives relating to the questions being studied. Different people may have their own version of the 'truth' and it may be hard to represent this diversity effectively.

Research requires evidence of *verisimilitude*, an accurate reflection of 'the truth'. We need to be aware of the dangers of reporting information without ensuring verisimilitude is achieved. In other words, we need to know that what we have established from people's accounts, verbal and written provides an accurate portrayal of a situation. Any political story in the media provides a good example of how different people's accounts can be. The role of the researcher is to find a way to obtain a 'picture' of 'facts' that is as close as possible to the way events actually occurred and the way a consensus of reasonable people might attempt objectively to represent them. A major division between research approaches occurs because of the way verisimilitude is understood. As noted in chapter 3, the scientific paradigm is based on the principle that there are universal laws that can be used to describe, predict and explain events. The laws exist. All we have to do is to work towards discovering them. We create hypotheses, test them and identify if our hypotheses can be refuted or substantiated.

Relativism

A different research approach, or paradigm, is based on the idea that there is no one single 'take' on an event: that it can be perceived differently by different people. At one level, each view is as accurate as any another, just as any person has as much right to exist as any other. This concept of relativism does, however, sometimes become highly problematic in research situations for a variety of reasons.

Can we really accept all views on a matter as having equal status? In an ideal world, this should be the case, but what about people who have fanatical and dangerous beliefs? There is a paradox here involved in the concept of freedom. We want to acknowledge all ideas and beliefs, but on the other hand, we may have to limit freedoms in situations in which dangerous views can harm other people. The determination of what is 'dangerous' can also be problematic, however, and may be highly political. Agreement on such ideas generally needs to rely on a consensus of evidence, commonly-held principles and views of what is 'reasonable'. Yet commonly-held views are also not always necessarily right! The difficulty with relativism, then, is that we cannot always use it effectively when we have to make decisions on behalf of groups of people. Sometimes we simply need to come to one overall consensus view that is practical and effective.

One way around the difficulty of dealing with a number of views is to plan to obtain them in the first place! Instead of avoiding the issue, why not meet it head on? If we want to know why some young people do not go on to further education and training, then we can ask them, their parents and guardians, their school teachers, college admission tutors, careers advisors and education guidance workers. Each group is likely to have a different perspective on our research question, but of course, in reality, they are all part of the issue we are examining. We are more likely to obtain an accurate picture of what is happening if we plan to ask all of these groups, rather than to rely solely on the perspective of the young people. We cannot possibly talk to every single person from every single group, so we then have to make decisions about how many people we will ask to participate in our research. How to make this decision is covered later in chapter 10.

Use of control groups

If you decide to use an experimental methodology, in which you want to test out a new teaching and learning method, for example, then what will you do about those who do not have the chance to participate? Your new method may be very effective. By working with one group of learners and not another, you may disadvantage the group that is not receiving the better method. On the other hand, you will not know if your method is better if you do not have a way of comparing it.

When planning research, it is important to remember what steps you should take to ensure that people have an equal opportunity to engage in a new practice. Often, you can ask for volunteers. Those who choose not to volunteer have every right to do so. Those who do volunteer can be advised of what they are letting themselves in for. A different approach is to ensure that the control group is given the new method under test after the comparison has been conducted.

Carrying out observations

If you decide that you want to observe an event, or behaviour in different settings, you are invariably changing the situation that you observe. The presence of strangers sitting in a room with a notebook or video cameras will be felt by those you are observing. You could decide to use hidden cameras, or one-way mirrors, but should you do this without people's consent? We are continually monitored by closed circuit television (CCTV) in our daily lives and we know that information derived from these helps catch criminals. We do not give permission for such monitoring. It is a different story if you plan to undertake research. People should not become sources of research without being asked to give their permission, although watching people in a public place is not a crime. There is a distinction between taking photographs of people in a college library, for example, and what you do with the pictures.

If you are unsure about the ethical issue concerning observation, make sure that you have followed guidelines, for example those set out by BERA. A good principle is to ask for permission to observe, explain what the purpose is and to negotiate how the findings of the observation will be made available to those being observed. In most colleges, staff are observed by line managers and professional development tutors as part of quality assurance or accredited programmes of training. The learners are informed that the focus of such observation is the member of staff, not them. This is an appropriate way to ensure that all those involved are aware of the parameters of the observation being conducted. You may find that you will wish to use a similar approach if you are observing a group of tutors and their practices, or your learners.

Ethical dilemmas

Research is an ethical minefield. We are dealing with people's lives and making use of the information that they provide. We therefore need ways to ensure we limit the damage we can do. One way to achieve this is to establish and adhere to the kinds of codes of good practice in research that the organisations listed above such as BERA, QCA and DfES, have created. Researchers working in FE could establish a code of good practice in research for their own regional group or local college based on these guidelines, and could set up a local or regional research ethics group to develop and discuss issues arising from this.

However, there will inevitably also be times when researchers will be faced with difficult decisions in local research situations that go beyond the specifications of any particular code. For example, participants often disclose very private and personal information during an interview. You may hear two conflicting sides of a story. You may hear something that you think should be reported elsewhere. What do you do if someone 'confesses' to a dependence on drugs to help them get through the day, or is showing signs of mental fatigue or breakdown? What if you interview people who are committing offences? If you do nothing, are you an accomplice to their crimes? What if you have reason to believe that someone is likely to harm him or herself? What is your role in such situations? You are not a counsellor or religious advisor, and you cannot, and should not, try to deal with such issues. If you decide that you do need to take action, one way is to say to the individual concerned that you are worried, or believe that it is necessary to do something and to ask their permission to do so.

If you are working on a qualification with a research component, you will have a supervisor. This person may be able to help you identify the best course of action in such circumstances. Dilemmas by their very nature do not have easy solutions. If you can share your situation with a colleague or supervisor, then you will have an opportunity to explore a variety of avenues. It is always better to seek advice than to carry on with your burden alone.

We remember a student working towards her EdD. She had been interviewing older people about their reminiscences of the second world war. One interviewee had become very dependent on her, expecting friendship and telephoning her many times each week. This person was clearly lonely. How could the student find a way to withdraw from this situation without causing distress to the old person? We are aware of this scenario because the EdD programme used a web-based discussion facility to support the students. By posting up her difficulty, other students and supervisors were able to engage in dialogue about ways and means to deal with this situation. This is one way in which a satisfactory solution might eventually be found for such a dilemma. Engaging the help of other participants in a research student support group or community of practitioners can enable us confidentially to share many such potential ethical research dilemmas in a safe atmosphere.

Finding out more:

Alasuutari, P. (1998) *An Invitation to Social Research* London: Sage Publications Ltd. (compares the work of the social researcher with that of detectives, examines issues of knowledge and power, observation and participation in social research).

Cohen, L., Manion, L., and Morrison, K. (2000) (5th edn) *Research Methods in Education* London: Routledge (particularly useful examination of ethics questions)

Ryan, A.B. (2001) *Feminist ways of knowing: towards theorising the person for radical adult education* Leicester: NIACE (questions of human subjectivity, discourse and feminism)

Section Three
Collecting Data
Some key methods

Chapter 8
Interviews and focus groups

Interviewing

Interviews are very pervasive in our society. We watch government officials, pop stars and members of studio audiences being interviewed on television. We hear people being interviewed on the radio. We read interviews in newspapers and magazines. Interviews occur when one person asks another a series of questions and therefore facilitates a discussion about an event or a topic. Interviews have many purposes. Police interview suspects to find out if they can gather evidence to arrest them. Television presenters interview pop stars and actors to help publicise a new release or new performance. Newspaper reporters interview people to provide information about their lives, or about activities that have been in the national or local news. Interviews can take place in formal settings and be recorded, such as in television and radio studios, offices and public institutions. They can take place in people's homes, in public parks, in the street. Very few people in this country have not seen, heard or taken part in an interview of one form or another in their lives.

Not all interviews have a research focus. The interview that takes place when someone is hoping to obtain a job, involves one person, the interviewer, finding out about another, the candidate or applicant. Interviews have a variety of forms and much can be learnt from observing interviews that are not used for research purposes. Let us look as some types of interview.

Structured interviews

In a structured interview, the interviewer has planned in advance what she or he wants to ask. There are questions set out on an interview schedule. The interview may be part of a large study and it is important that all participants are asked the same questions, to ensure validity within the research. The significant feature of a structured interview is that the control lies primarily with the interviewer. The questions are predetermined, and therefore the interviewer knows in advance what will be asked. The interviewee may be informed beforehand what the questions will be, and can prepare answers to them, something which is particularly important if the interviewer wants information that has to be obtained from documents, reports and management information systems. The interviewer may recite the questions at the beginning of the interview, and then proceed through them one by one in a set order. The interviewer may begin with the first question and work through them, and the respondent will simply react to them as they are asked.

Structured interviews are particularly useful when the point of the research is to focus down on a particular topic. They can help test out findings from different research previously undertaken, or from a preliminary survey. They can be used to summarise and confirm previous information.

Structured interviews do, however, run the risk of not tapping into reservoirs of knowledge and information that the interviewee may unknowingly possess. If the interviewer does not ask a question, the interviewee won't have an opportunity to say something on that matter. The danger of not finding out about important aspects of the topic under investigation can be quite serious. A common example occurs when a researcher talks to a group of 'socially excluded' people such as drug users, or offenders. The drug users may be reluctant to discuss aspects of their behaviour and because the interview schedule is focusing on one aspect of their lives, perhaps their use of needles, they do not have to talk about how they obtain their drugs. Yet the latter may be far more important to know about if the research is trying to establish ways to help drug users 'kick' their habit.

On the other hand, structured interviews are useful when interviewees are either too reticent or too talkative. The researcher can move on to the next question, either as a way of closing down a meandering response which is going off at a tangent to the issue under consideration, or as a way of encouraging an interviewee to talk some more. This is also very handy if the interviewer has forgotten what to ask next!

Name

Course

Date of joining college

How many GCSEs do you have

What subjects are they

When did you obtain them

What qualifications are you hoping to achieve this year?

What are you planning to do after you finish at college this year?

Have you had any careers guidance from the college?

If yes, have you found the guidance helpful?

If no, have you gone for any guidance outside of the college?

If so, where?

Thank you for taking part in the interview.

Figure 8.1: Structured Interview

Semi-structured interviews

One way round interviews that are too tightly structured is to devise a set of questions and then allow opportunities for the interviewee to add ideas and points that may not have been initially thought of by the interviewer. Often, semi-structured interviews will have a set of themes that the interviewer will address, with prompts to help the interviewee if the first response is rather limited. The advantage of a semi-structured interview is that there is still an agenda to keep the interview 'on track' but there is more free flow discussion, which can help the interviewer find out about other aspects from the interviewee's perspective, and explore avenues which have not been previously determined.

The disadvantage of a semi-structured interview is that an interviewee may go off at such a tangent that it changes the nature of the interview.

Name
Course
Date of joining college?
How many GCSEs do you have?
What subjects are they?
When did you obtain them?
What qualifications are you hoping to achieve this year?

We are interested in the choices you have made. Can you tell us a little bit about why you are taking the programmes you have just mentioned?

Tell me about the most helpful person when you were deciding what programmes to study here at the college.

Prompts:
Did you have any help from people in the college in making your choices?
Have you had help from people outside of the college in making your choices?

Have any of your friends used the services provided by the college? If so, what was their experience?

Is there anything else you would like to raise about your choice of programmes and how you decided what to do?

Thank you for taking part in the interview.

Figure 8.2: Semi Structured Interview

Unstructured interviews

Unstructured interviews are more like conversations. There may be an overall focus, or topic under consideration. However, instead of an interviewer setting an agenda and a series of questions, the dialogue in an unstructured interview is free flowing. Unstructured interviews are useful when the nature of the topic is still being explored, and different understandings of that topic are required. They are also useful if the interviewee is an expert in the field, and is able to draw upon considerable experience in covering the topic, much of which the interviewer may be unaware. With an unstructured interview, the power relationship is more evenly spread between interviewer and interviewee.

The disadvantage of an unstructured interview is that the conversation may completely wander off the topic under investigation, or be dominated by the agenda of the interviewee, or comprise a rambling discussion that does not fully explore anything. Great skill is required in facilitating unstructured interviews. Very few people actually conduct an unstructured interview even if they think they do. Most people have some agenda, even if it has not been written down. Those who are skilful in interviewing may control the interview in subtle ways and the structure, although not initially apparent, underpins the flow of conversation.

Name

Course

We are interested in how people make choices for the programmes they study. could you tell us how you went about it?

Figure 8.3: Unstructured Interview

Asking questions

Many people think it is easy to ask questions. When they devise an interview schedule, they expect their interviewee to be able to respond to their questions without any difficulty. Yet one person's idea of an easy question may be incomprehensible to another. Let us look at an example of interview questions. Suppose we want to know about people's experience of crime in the last year, or more importantly, their perception of crime. In fact, this kind of interview is conducted annually on behalf of the police force. It often shows that people's perceptions of crime, in particular their fear of crime, actually outweighs the incidence of crime. Let us assume that we have a group of people in a local estate. We want to find out about why very few of them come to the college in the evenings for the community education programme. We think it may be because people are reluctant to go out in the evenings because of their concern for their personal safety. We have decided to ask them about their experience of crime.

Look at this list of questions

- Have you experienced crime in the last year?

- Can you tell me about it?

- Did you report it to the police?

- What happened?

- Has it made any difference to you?

Now let us think of someone who has not had any personal experience of crime in the last year. The answer to the first question will be 'no'. The rest of the questions are then redundant. However, this person may be so worried about being attacked, that she hardly ever goes out, even in the daytime. Knowing what she thinks about crime would help us identify ways to make her feel safe. But our interview questions will have yielded nothing.

A further concern about our questions is that we may interview someone who has just experienced an extremely traumatic personal attack. We may unwittingly cause this person great distress in our questioning. We cannot know that our questions will set off any number of emotional responses, but we must be aware that this can happen and be prepared to deal with them. We should be aware that some questions will lead to emotional responses that require careful handling.

Let us try again with some different questions.

- Some people say that there is so much crime these days that they do not feel safe in the streets. Is this something you would agree with?

- Have you any examples of this? (personal, family, friends, neighbours?)

- When you go out, for example to the shops, how do you get there?

- Are there times of the day when you would not go out?

- Why is this?

- Can you give an example of what you did when you did have to go out at a time you do not like to go out?

- How did you feel?

With the second set of questions, there is scope for the person answering to give examples, not just of personal experiences but of those of people known to her. She can agree or disagree with a general statement, and by doing so, can be asked to give reasons, all of which will begin to reveal her perceptions of the issue.

The way in which questions are asked, then, help to provide either full responses, or confirm or refute statements. Questions which are designed to help people give their opinion or describe a situation are known as *open questions*. They are aimed at stimulating discussion. They often start with phrases such as 'tell me about', 'in what ways?' 'can you describe?'. Sometimes you will want to check that you have understood what has been said. Here, *closed questions* are useful. These are phrased in such a way that people answer yes or no to them. They start with phrases like 'have you?' 'do you?' 'are you?'. There is nothing wrong with using closed questions to confirm a response but they are not usually a good idea at the start of an interview.

You will also want to find a way to 'settle' someone into the interview. Telling the interviewee what you are hoping to find out, how long it should take, ensuring confidentiality and agreeing whether the interviewee will have an opportunity to make comments on any transcript is a good way to begin an interview, as it defines the context and helps the interviewee concentrate on the issue at hand. You may then wish to ask questions about the person, perhaps to know about age, experience, why this person is in a particular situation and so forth. Only then can you begin to ask about the issue you are researching. If you start with far too open a question, the person may wander off the topic and it will be hard for you to bring the interview back to your focus. Many interviews involve a gradual opening of the discussion through open questions, and then a gradual closing down, using more closed questions. You may find you wish to use a more cyclical process, with open and closed questions following on from each other.

Pilot

Do not assume that your first set of questions will work out well! We have worked with teachers and trainers of adults for some years now, and when they try out interviews on each other before they use them in their own research, they always comment on how dreadful their questions were, even though they had worked on them with small groups beforehand. You can have a lot of fun designing questions, but do remember to pilot them. This means trying them out on a small group of people who will not be taking part in your research, but who will be able to respond to the questions as though they were your chosen interviewees. You can then refine any questions that did not work, or were misleading. Then, you must pilot again, so that your revised questions have been tested, too. Many people assume that having changed their first set of questions, the second set must be better. Only when you are sure that your second set of questions work should you use them in your research.

Places where interviews are conducted

So far, the types of interviews discussed have focused on how much structure there is to the questioning, linked with how much control the interviewer has over the situation. The next consideration is whether the interviews will be conducted face to face, or through other forms of communication media. With all interviews, it is important to recognise that where an interview is conducted affects the power dimension. For example, if you are hoping to interview your college principal, it is highly unlikely that this will take place in the student coffee shop! Often, people who hold senior posts within organisations expect that an interviewer will come to their office, or meet at a location which is chosen by them. This means that the interviewer is on someone else's territory, and this immediately places the power relationship in the interviewee's favour. This is not an issue where there is a wrong or right, but it does mean that there may be practical consequences that follow from where interviews are held.

Imagine settling down to begin your semi-structured interview schedule and the principal's administrator interrupts to say that the chair of governors is outside and wishes to speak to the principal as a matter of urgency. If you are in the principal's office, it is very difficult to ask that you be uninterrupted, although courtesy would usually demand that the principal treat your appointment as being as important as the next person's. However, the realities of working in a very complex and busy sector such as further education dictates that there are going to be priorities that a principal must respond to. If, on the other hand, the principal had agreed to come to your office (assuming that you have one and that it is not shared by colleagues), then you are in a position to ensure that you will not be interrupted and that telephone calls will not be answered and preferably diverted. There is nothing worse than trying to ask searching questions with a phone ringing, an answerphone recorded message playing, or being interrupted whilst your interviewee answers the phone. Remember, you are asking people to give up their time to talk to you, and you are not in a position to dictate that they give you their sole attention. You could ask them if it is possible to find a room where you can be uninterrupted and have quiet, and space, to talk confidentially.

Not all interviews are best conducted in formal settings like offices. Sometimes, people will feel far more relaxed and willing to talk if they are out of the hurly burly of their workplace. You may find that you can visit people in their homes, or in more neutral public places such as hotel lobbies and cafes. You will need to be careful about your own personal safety if interviewing in places which are unfamiliar to you. Always leave a note with a colleague, friend or family member stating where you are and what time you expect to return.

Interviewing in people's homes is not always plain sailing. Years ago, one of us was interviewing colleagues about their basic education practice, and found herself in the kitchen of one part time tutor, discussing practice with her and being continually interrupted by her husband, who had just been on a volunteer training programme and was very enthusiastic about joining in. It was not easy to find a way to ask him to leave us alone, and unfortunately, the part time tutor being interviewed did not seem to think it was a difficulty. You may be interrupted by children or animals (or both!), and again, people being interviewed may want to answer the phone when it rings because, quite rightly, it is their home and they are giving up time to talk to you. One of the longest interviews we conducted took four hours in total, with our conversation being interrupted by the tutor's four teenage children, telephone, time out for coffee and nibbles. The resulting interview showed no sign of suffering from the interruptions, but the interviewer was exhausted by the end of the evening!

Seating arrangements
One of the factors which affects the way people interact is the type of seating arrangement and how much formality this represents. You may find that people want to be interviewed from behind their desks,

with you very much in a subordinate position seated opposite. You may be able to control the way you interview by placing chairs at an angle to the corner of a desk, which allows for maximum eye contact without imposing an 'inquisitorial' feel to the procedure. Some people feel comfortable with a desk or table by their side. In unusual circumstances, you may even find that you can interview someone when you are both standing. This at least limits the time you will spend in the interview, as most people cannot stand up for too long!

Timing of interviews

When you arrange an interview, you need to think about the time of day when this will be conducted. If you interview people at the end of a long, busy, day, it is likely that both of you will be tired and less able to concentrate. On the other hand, some people are not at their best first thing in the morning, or they may have many demands on their time and will not be able to give you long enough for you to ask all the questions you have prepared. People need to feel comfortable, and if they are near a meal time, they may not concentrate if they are feeling hungry, or thirsty. These seem rather trivial points to make, but people really do behave differently according to their body rhythms. You will also need to take account of people's other responsibilities. If you set your interviews for late in the afternoon, some people may have childcare considerations and will be anxious to get away as soon as possible. It is helpful if you are holding an interview at your office, or in a room that you have booked, to have water available. You may be able to offer a hot drink. This all helps people relax and feel more comfortable. It is also a considerate and professional way to conduct an interview.

Note taking and recording

Once you have decided on what you want to ask, and where you are going to do it, you now need to think about how you will keep a record of what was being said. A common way to record an interview is to use a tape recorder. You must always ask permission to record someone's comments. Some people may find a recorder intrusive and be wary of what they say. Others will enjoy having the attention and be very keen to talk profusely. It is not easy to have a tape recorder recording unobtrusively, although the range of equipment available today is such that there are numerous facilities, including voice activated recorders, and microphones which clip on to people's clothing, rather than being placed ostentatiously in front of the interviewee. If you are going to record an interview, then it is vital that you try out the equipment beforehand, and that you undertake a 'voice check' with your interviewee. This can be off putting for both of you, as you then have to hear your voices. However, it is essential to check that the voice level is being recorded. Even when you have done this, keep an eye on your tape recorder. I once undertook the voice check with an interviewee, played it back and started the interview but forgot to press the record button second time around. It is so easy to forget to press a button when you are trying to sort out your notes, relax the interviewee and gather your thoughts.

Even if you do record, you should think about keeping some skeleton notes during the interview. At least if your recorder does let you down, you have some idea of what was said. Try not to spend the whole interview looking down at your notes. Eye contact is extremely important here. You are also going to notice body language if you keep eye contact with your interviewee. You do need to respect another person's space and in some cultures, looking directly at a person's eyes is considered highly insolent. If your interviewee does not want to look at you, then that is acceptable and there is little you can do about it. Remember, if you are interviewing your own students, you are in a position of power, not only because you are asking them to talk to you, but because you are their tutor. Not everyone will be happy to talk to you and they may show this non-verbally in their body language.

When you take notes, remember to ask your interviewee if that is acceptable. In some situations, you may find that it is going to be difficult to take notes and you may have to rely on your recorder. It may be helpful to have a list of your questions with gaps for responses, so that you can take notes in a more structured way. You may also find it helpful to write additional information on your notes before you start, such as date, name of interviewee, place of interview, time interview started and finished, and if there were any interruptions. Always have at least one spare pen, and preferably some pencils, so that you can continue note taking if your pen stops working.

You may want to make a video recording of your interview. This does give you both a verbal and visual record. However, video recorders may feel even more intrusive to your interviewee. Again, you will need to check that the equipment is working and you will have to consider where to place the video camera and how this will affect the dynamic of the interview. As with many research methods, interviewing introduces an element of contrivance into a situation and great care must be made when analysing the data, as an interview is not a natural situation for many respondents.

Telephone interviews

All the examples discussed so far involve interviewing people face to face. It may not be possible to arrange to meet with your selected interviewees. College staff are incredibly busy and are often unable to find an hour in their working day to meet for an interview. If you are hoping to meet people who are physically dispersed, it is time consuming for you to travel to meet them, or vice versa. One acceptable method of interviewing that has developed over the last few years is telephone interviewing. You can arrange to contact your interviewee by telephone at a set time and conduct your interview over the phone. It is possible to record such an interview, again with the interviewee's permission. You will not have the additional information gained from watching your interviewee's body language, but you may at least hold an interview which otherwise would be impossible to set up.

If you are going to conduct an interview by telephone, it is even more important that you create some structure to the process. Telephone calls can be quite costly and the more prepared your interviewee is, the more likely you will be given answers to your questions as you ask them. You may find sending your questions ahead of time a useful way to facilitate the telephone conversation. As you conduct the interview, you will need to take notes, even if you have permission to record the interview. At least you do not have to maintain eye contact with telephone interviews.

Web based interviews

These days, you do not even need to establish personal, synchronous contact with your interviewee. You can conduct interviews electronically, either synchronously or asynchronously using the internet. Here, you post up your questions and ask people to respond to them. This way of interviewing becomes much closer to conducting surveys, as discussed in chapter 9. However, with an interview, you are offering people a chance to express their views verbally, without asking them to tick answer boxes or rate their views numerically.

With web based interviews, it is important to establish when you are asking people to provide responses, and how you will ensure confidentiality. If you have a separate email address, this is fairly easy to assure. However, if you are using a more interactive website, then you will need to establish what is going to happen to the responses and whether these will be viewed by other participants in your interviews.

Group interviews

In some situations, it is actually desirable for a group of people to be interviewed. You may find that some reticent people will feel more able to speak if they are with a group of their peers. You may be wanting to gain a perception of a particular issue that could be facilitated by a form of brainstorming, where people 'bounce' ideas off each other and one view stimulates ideas from others in the group. There are as many ways to conduct group interviews as individual interviews, and all the methods of communication, face to face, telephone and web based can be used. In addition, if you have the facility, video conferencing is a good way to engage a group of people who live a great distance from each other but can be brought together to discuss an issue at a set moment in time.

Sharing virtual discussions using video or web conferencing facilities is a useful method of electronic interaction and collaboration. It can be technically complex to set up both video and web conferencing, but in some instances it may be worth the time and trouble for a particular research project that requires it. There are many specialist private firms and educational institutions providing help with both video and web conferencing for a fee. If the use of collaborative interviews through video or web conferencing is essential to your project, it might be helpful to cost this into your project. Many higher education institutions have video and web conferencing facilities, and you may be able to arrange to use these facilities for a cost-effective price. In the planning of your research, it will be helpful to work out precisely which technical system you are going to use well in advance of the scheduled discussions. It's also useful to set aside time to test the facilities in advance using a 'mock' group interview session before the real interviews. It will be important to get a technically-competent person to assist you on the day of your group discussions in case anything goes wrong.

Focus Groups

A specific form of group interviews is the focus group. The process arose from market research, in which people would be invited to give their views on certain products. More recently, focus groups have been used by politicians, to identify which policies are popular, or to take account of the 'general public' when forming policy. Focus groups require good preparation. Focus groups do not work with large numbers of people. Usually eight to ten people are best. Focus groups do not have to be like market research where you ensure that you have a representative sample from across the population. In fact, focus groups are particularly useful when you have want to find out the views of a particular group from society, for example, young single mothers. They may be prepared to talk about why they have not come to a college to learn if they know that the other people in their group are going to have the same situation. Focus groups can be used to help people articulate ideas that they many not have had the opportunity to think about. One person in the group may say something that sparks off ideas from other members. They may agree, or disagree.

The skill of the focus group facilitator is in managing what people say. There are numerous ways to do this. You may decide that you have some statements that you want people to respond to. You could put these on flipchart paper and ask people to write their ideas underneath. You may decide that you do not want to embarrass people who are not willing to write in public. In this way, you may have pre-prepared cards which you ask people to place under certain headings. This system helps you to categorise people's views about something. For example, you may want to know what factors prevent people from coming to college. If you wrote down a list of topics such as 'no bus' 'creche too expensive for me' 'no time' and then asked people to put these statements in the order they consider to affect their decision about not coming to college, then you may begin to identify a trend. Now, when you put the individual responses to the whole group, you may find that you can gain consensus about the main contributing factor to non-participation in learning at the college by this particular group. If you conduct a number of focus groups, you may begin to obtain valuable insights into what stops people from coming to the college. If you had asked people individually, they may have provided answers that did not really give you such depth. It is through dialogue that people begin to explain why they perceive things and they can help you reach an understanding from their viewpoint.

Researcher: Just to get us started, in pairs, please take five minutes to tell each other your name and one piece of information about yourself.

Each person then introduces the partner.

Researcher: We would like you to tell us about your reasons for returning to study at our college. Now, there are probably loads of reasons, so here are some yellow 'stickies'. Please write all the reasons that you feel contributed to you deciding to return to learn. Please put each reason on a separate sticky. When you have finished, please put them up on this flipchart

After this activity, researcher and participants view the reasons

The researcher then begins to place reasons together, perhaps in themes. For example, there may be a number of 'stickies' stating that people wanted to change career, or begin a career.

There may be a further set that relate to 'getting the brain going again'

The researcher places these in sets, and confirms with the participants whether this makes sense. Throughout the focus group, the participants discuss their views, all of which is recorded.

The researcher could even begin to develop a hierarchy, finding the reasons which are most important, or which contributed most to people's decision to return to learning at the college.

As a result of this, there is a consensus about the different reasons, and all of this has come as a result of discussion and careful facilitation of the group.

Figure 8.4: Example of a focus group process

The dynamic in a focus group is an important consideration. In any group setting, there will be people who are very forthright and have no difficulty in expressing their views. There will be people who are silent, or who feel uncomfortable expressing their views publicly. You must therefore think of using a variety of strategies to maximise their participation. You can ask people to write ideas down individually, to talk in pairs, to vote for particular statements, make decisions about whether one statement is more important than another, as well as asking people to sit around and 'brainstorm' in one large group.

Gaining access to interviewees

Throughout this book, we talk about obtaining permission to conduct your research. You cannot just go off and conduct a set of interviews without first ensuring that you are permitted to do so. If you want to interview your learners, just because you are their tutor does not mean that you do not have to ask permission from your institution.

Not only do you require permission to conduct your interviews. You may need to gain access to people you wish to talk to. If you are undertaking a comparison of learners in different institutions, perhaps a college, and adult education institution and a training provider, then you will have to negotiate access to groups of people. It helps if you can be clear at the outset what your research is about and why you wish to talk to the individuals concerned. You may have to rely on an intermediary to help you gain the permission you require. It is important to identify the appropriate person to approach. Try to write a formal letter of request and then follow this up with a personal approach by telephone.

You may find that the best way to approach people is to ask a senior member within the organisation for permission to send requests to the people you wish to talk to through *their* systems of communication, for which they are responsible. For example, you may produce a flyer which asks people to come forward to talk to you about their experiences of studying as mature students. You can approach the programme manager for a number of curriculum areas and ask if it is possible for your leaflet to be distributed by the tutors concerned.

Provided you have already gained permission from the institution, and can show this to the programme managers, then they are likely to co-operate. Remember to ensure that your contact details are available for any volunteers who wish to be interviewed.

Even if you decide that you are going to use the web for interviewing, it is important to ensure that you have permission to conduct your research before posting a general request for participants. Although there is less 'policing' on the web, and certainly there is nothing to stop you creating your own personal website and hoping that you will have enough 'hits' to provide you with participants, if you wish to act professionally, and certainly if you are using your institution's website address, then you must ensure that you are acting within institution and legal frameworks.

This protocol of requesting permission protects you, too. If someone did want to complain about being approached, or about you being within a certain institution and talking to individuals, you can provide evidence that you are there legitimately. With the need for increased security, the chances are that you will not gain access physically to premises without evidence that you have been invited to be there.

Confidentiality

One of the key factors in conducting interviews is the issue of confidentiality, which we explored in chapter 7. It is best to assume that all participants should be guaranteed confidentiality and only with their permission should you deviate from this rule.

Analysing data

Never underestimate the time it takes to analyse interview transcripts. One, hour long interview can take approximately six hours to transcribe and analyse. You may be lucky enough to use shorthand, but most people have to painstakingly listen to a tape, stop it and write down what was said, and carry on listening to the next part. You may be able to type directly onto a word processor, but even this can take time.

When you transcribe your first tape, you will probably want to write down every single utterance made. When you come to read through your transcript, you will find that both interviewer and interviewee appear to be remarkably inept at speaking! It is only when you see in writing what people actually say that you realise that people, most of the time, do not speak in sentences, and often leave words unsaid, repeat what they say, stumble and interject with particular phrases, words or noises. You will probably decide after this first experience not to write down every single utterance, but to write down the main points!

You may find it helpful to use different pens for your words and those of your interviewee. If typing, you may use a different font, or use bold or italic to help differentiate between the two speakers.

If you have recorded a group interview, you will need to be even clearer in identifying the different speakers. Colour coding may help you here. With a video, you will need to watch it many times, identifying points on the tape where you wish to make particular reference to a response of your interviewee, and you will also need to transcribe what they have said. With web interviews, at least you have an electronic record of people's responses.

You may find that there are parts of your tape recording that you simply cannot make sense of. Your interviewee may have turned away from the microphone and the words will be inaudible. You may be able to ask your interviewee for clarification, particularly if you have agreed that you will send them the transcript after the interview. If not, then you may be able to make out what was said from the context of the sentence. However, do *not* put your own words in. If you do not have the information, then leave a blank. Remember, it is your interviewee's words that are the focus of your attention here, not your version of them. You will have the opportunity to distil their words through your analysis in the next part of the process.

Once you have created your records and transcripts, you now must begin your analysis. It is worth spending time listening to your tapes and reading through your transcripts at least twice before you decide how you will analyse them. This is an important part of the process. You need to immerse yourself in the data and allow the data to provide you with insights and ideas of potential categories or themes.

This process is particularly used with the grounded theory approach (Glaser and Strauss, 1967, Strauss and Corbin, 1990). Here, you do not have predetermined codes that you are applying, but you are searching the data to allow it to show you likely themes. If your interview is structured, then you clearly have a set number of categories that you can apply directly. However, people's responses may throw up new themes, or the way in which they responded may be analysed in different ways.

Let us return to our example of Mandy's investigation into retention in chapter 4. She used a semi-structured interview schedule. She has transcribed each tape so that she has a written record. She has listened to each tape twice, and has spent a lot of time rewinding and listening to these whilst creating the transcripts. She can begin to identify some key issues arising from the data.

The first step is for Mandy to read each transcript and highlight responses which appear to relate to one of her key issues. She can go through each of the transcripts in turn, highlighting this one issue. Then, she can go through them looking for her second issue, and highlighting the responses accordingly. At the end of this process, Mandy will have a patchwork of colour on each of her transcripts, each colour relating to one of the themes that she has identified. It is vital at this point to remember that the themes that are emerging are Mandy's ideas, not those of her interviewees. She is synthesising and analysing the data and putting her own interpretation on what has been said. The raw data, the transcripts, are now being turned into analysis and findings.

Once Mandy has identified all the themes that she feels have emerged from the data, she must now go back to the raw data and check that her ideas really do hold up on second inspection. This is a key part of the process. Sometimes, people develop ideas about themes and look for them so carefully that they miss other important issues. They may also 'skew' their reading of the data to fit their own ideas of themes and categories. One way to help mediate against this bias is for other people to be asked to read through the data and to see if they code the responses in the same way.

Software for interview analysis

There are computer programmes which can analyse transcripts. The more commonly used ones are Nu-Dist and Atlas-Ti. You do not have to have this software to analyse the data, but they enable you to provide a more careful analysis, and of course, they take far less time than reading through and coding everything manually. With the software, you create a set of codes which you believe capture the characteristics of the data. If you are not sure of the meaning of some of your codes then you can write additional information in a memo which is attached to each code, and this can also remind you to link them up with other codes or issues as you go through the data. Once you have coded your data, it is then possible to search for groups or 'families'. It is at this stage that the software is most effective. With Atlas-Ti, it is possible to create networks or 'nodes' which show relationships between the codes, and you can create sophisticated analyses of your data as a result.

However, such software is only as good as its users. Over reliance on software which allows you to identify commonly occurring words will not usually capture the intensity of statements, and this is where the tape recordings or video recordings have their advantages.

Once you have coded your data, you must check that your codes do apply throughout, in other words, that they have 'goodness of fit'. Strauss and Corbin (1990) call the process of checking that the data fits the emerging themes as 'saturation of the categories'. In other words, you have read through your transcripts, and coded them, checked that your coding holds up to another person's analysis of the same raw data, and that re-analysing the data does not provide you with any different themes or categories.

Now you will be in a position to write your analysis of the interviews. Again, do not underestimate the time it takes to sift through your data, create your themes or categories and then decide how you will record this. A really useful book by Orna and Stephens (1996) provides information about how to manage the information that you have got. If you were to write a report where you repeated every single word that your interviewees used, then it would be tiresome to read and inefficient for you to report. The important thing about writing up your analysis of interviews is for you to discuss the emerging themes but to use examples from your transcripts to illustrate a point you are making.

Supposing Mandy found that confidence was a key emerging theme from her interviews. She may find that within this large theme there are sub themes, such as initial confidence to return to learning, growing confidence and learners' awareness that they are tackling other issues in their lives as a result of this, and confidence to disagree with what they read in sessions. She could write a short introduction to the way in which confidence permeated all of the interviews. She could then state how she found different aspects of confidence. Then she could write about each subcategory. This is where examples from the interviewees' comments are useful. It helps the reader make sense of what Mandy has done in her analysis, and it supports Mandy's argument that this theme is a key theme from her research.

A danger with analysing interviews and reporting them is that the writer can get carried away by what has been said by interviewees. The statements are often so powerful, that the writer is tempted to put all of them in as examples. Ultimately, this dilutes the effect on the reader, and is a little sloppy as a form of analysis. It is hard to decide on which particular comment to include and which should be left out, but remember the process of interviewing moves from gaining enormous amounts of data to a summary of what has emerged from the analysis. It is impossible to ensure that every single participant is equally represented at this stage, and it is also vital to ensure that differences of opinion are reported and discussed.

When writing up the analysis, try very had to avoid 'weasel words'. Supposing Mandy stated that 'some learners did not feel at all threatened by the idea of coming to the further education college' this does not give us enough detail. Was it two, four or ten people? On the other hand, if Mandy decided that she wanted to express the number of people stating this view numerically, saying '50% of respondents did not feel at all threatened by the idea of coming to the further education college' is a little too statistical, given that she only talked to ten people. Percentages are best used for large numbers. In this case, she would be better stating that half the people stated that they were not threatened, and she could then explore why this was from their interviews, and also begin to discuss whether the other half had the opposite view, or simply had not mentioned it.

Once you have your transcripts, it is not always possible to go back to the interviewees to check out further thoughts, or clarify what they have said. If you realise that half of the people mentioned something but the other half did not, it would have been helpful if you could ask those that did not express a view, what they thought about it. Sometimes you can arrange to talk to someone again, particularly if you can telephone them to check things out with them.

A danger with interview analysis is paying too much attention to some aspects and missing, or playing down others. This is where you should ensure that you count the number of times something has been discussed within each interview and then identify how this compares with each of the other interviews. However, an issue raised only once by one person may be important, even if it is not frequently noted. You have to use your own judgement at this stage in the interview analysis, but remember that your reporting of your analysis enables others to judge for themselves whether your approach stands up to scrutiny. Many publicly reported interviews fall foul of bias, and many interviewees subsequently complain that they have been misrepresented. Your interviewees may not have such an opportunity.

Reporting your findings

You have to think about what happens to the reported conversation when you analyse your interviews. If you include quotes from the discussion, people reading the report may recognise the person from the type of quote given. You must ensure that you have permission to use the information gained from an interview. You could agree that the interviewee can read through your record and make any changes to the content. The interviewee may ask that you do not report certain comments. You must abide by the request, as the individual owns his or her words. As happens often in the public press, people's words are reported out of context. You must be very careful that you do not do this, and offering your respondents an opportunity to see what you have reported is another way to ensure that you have represented their views accurately.

Summary of interviews and focus groups

Interviews are useful for:

- Obtaining information about people's perceptions and experiences
- Gaining in depth information
- Discussing and sharing ideas

Interviews are time consuming:

- to prepare
- in terms of travel unless using telephone, video or web
- in recording and analysing

Interviews are:

- collaborative
- searching

Interviews can be difficult...

- if respondents are non-forthcoming
- if respondents are too vociferous
- if the interviewer does not ask appropriate questions

Interviews can be biased:

- in the questions asked
- in the responses given
- in the analysis
- in the reporting of the analysis

Finding out more:

Bell, J., and Opie, C. (2002) *Learning from Research: Getting more from your data* Buckingham: Open University Press

Cohen, L., Manion, L., and Morrison, K. (2000) (5th edn) *Research Methods in Education* London: Routledge

Gillham, B. (2000) *The Research Interview* London: Continuum

McNiff, J., Lomax, P., and Whitehead, J. (1996) *You and your Action Research Project* London: Routledge

Orna, E and Stevens, J. (1995) *Managing Information for Research* Buckingham: Open University Press

Strauss A., and Corbin, J.M.(1990) *Basic of Qualitative research: grounded theory procedures and techniques* London: Sage

Chapter 9
Questionnaires and surveys

It's a grey, cold Sunday afternoon. Hildi has fallen asleep by the fireplace over her questionnaire design again. Hildi is studying full-time, and is also a part-time FE maths and numeracy lecturer in Leicester, with teaching and marking to do. She therefore doesn't get as much time as she'd like to do her research. At the college where Hildi works, the adult and 16-18 year old students she teaches desperately need her help, so she doesn't skimp on either lesson preparation or marking. This leaves little time to do much studying for her post-graduate certificate in education course, and even less time to complete the work she needs to do for her dissertation. She enjoys her work on the initial teacher training course, but it's been hard-going this term.

Let us say, therefore, that Hildi has decided to design a questionnaire for a small survey with the research question, 'How satisfied are students with their programme of study at this campus?' She decides it will be useful to distribute this to all students during their lessons in the main college campus, using a coding system for the classes, so that she can see how her two classes compare with others in terms of their levels of satisfaction overall.

These are some basic things Hildi needs to think carefully about:

* what *exactly* does she want to find out in her research?

* is a questionnaire the best *method* of finding this out?

* is a survey the best research *strategy* to use?

- can *data collection* using this method be achieved in the time and resources?

- Will she follow up her survey with some *interviews* of volunteer respondents?

- is she able to *analyse* the results effectively using this method?

- are timing and resources sufficient to complete the analysis and *report results*?

In deciding this, she needs to recognise the following about questionnaires:

- there are benefits and disadvantages in using questionnaires

- very careful questionnaire design is needed, including a trial and pilot phase

- confidentiality and other ethical issues must be addressed

- the questionnaire must really ask the questions needed for the research

- questions must 'fit' with the audience's abilities and sensitivities

- language used should be clear and simple, not ambiguous

- resources to carry out the research must be planned in advance

- coding and analysis of questions must be planned at the design stage

- reporting of results should be linked back to the questions asked

Advantages of questionnaires – why choose this method?

There are some clear advantages that would benefit Hildi in considering the use of questionnaires, particularly *self-completed questionnaires,* in which learners are given the questions to be answered in written paper or on-line format. Learners then complete questionnaires in their own time and return the completed forms to the researcher. This method of collecting the views of learners is very efficient and useful as a time-saving method of carrying out research to gain the views of multiple people simultaneously.

We enclose below an example of a self-completed questionnaire from a real study carried out with funding from the LSDA in 2001-3. This study was carried out to research the question, '*What are FE teachers' perceptions of the effectiveness of initial training in helping them to teach and to support learning?*' The study made use of the key areas in teaching and supporting learning identified in the Further Education National Training Organisation (FENTO) standards for teaching (FENTO 1999). Drawing upon results from this questionnaire, the researchers conducted follow up telephone interviews over the two phases of the project.

The results of this questionnaire are reported in the publication, *Recollected in tranquillity? FE teachers' perceptions of their initial teacher training* (Harkin, Clow and Hillier, 2003). We have included this research example, with the permission of the researchers, as it is an instance of a recent self-completed questionnaire distributed to FE practitioners, as part of a process of improving capacity for research by FE teachers.

In the same time as it would take to do one interview, survey questionnaires can be completed by large numbers of learners, systematically collecting significant amounts of useful quantitative data. Data can also be anonymously collected in a survey, allowing respondents to report potentially sensitive information that may not emerge in some other situations. Factual evidence as well as opinions and values of a large number of people can be reported simultaneously in straightforward process.

If the questionnaire process is well-designed in a reliable and valid way, the results can be very effective in providing compelling evidence. Therefore, if Hildi has little time, she might find that the use of self-completed questionnaires such as the one we have included here is particularly useful as a method in her situation. As she may be working on her own with only a small amount of resources, she could scale down her project into just one main survey phase, with questionnaires distributed to a smaller number of students than in the example here, and follow-up interviews with selected volunteers.

Appendix 1: the questionnaire

The effectiveness of initial training in improving teachers' ability to teach and support learning in FE – your perceptions

learning and skills development agency

Please use black ink when completing this questionnaire, to aid electronic scanning, and mark boxes like this

Q1 The subject which I MAINLY teach would BEST be described as being in the category of
(tick one only)

☐ Sciences (incl. maths and computing)
☐ Agriculture
☐ Construction
☐ Engineering (incl. manufacturing)
☐ Business

☐ Hotel & Catering (incl. leisure and tourism)
☐ Health & Community (incl. hairdressing)
☐ Art & Design (incl. media and performing arts)
☐ Humanities
☐ Basic Education
☐ Other (*please specify below*)

Q2 The age of students which I MAINLY teach would BEST be described as being
(tick one only)

☐ 16–19 year olds   ☐ Over 19 years old

Q3 The type of qualification on which I MAINLY teach would BEST be described as
(tick one only)

☐ General/Academic (such as GCSE/A Level)
☐ General Vocational (such as GNVQ or BTEC)
☐ Vocational/Occupational (such as NVQ)
☐ Access to HE
☐ Professional Qualifications

Q4 I am in the following age group

☐ 21–35   ☐ 36–45   ☐ 46–55   ☐ Over 55

Q5 I am

☐ Male   ☐ Female

Q6 In this college I work

☐ Full-time   ☐ Part-time fractional   ☐ Part-time hourly paid

Q7 I have been teaching in the Further Education sector for

☐ years

Figure 9.1: Example questionnaire (Harkin, Clow and Hillier, 2003)

Q8 **I have these initial FE teaching qualifications** *(please tick the relevant boxes and insert dates)*

CG7306

CG7307   Start date [   ]   Completion date [   ]

PG/CertEd (FE)   Start date [   ]   Completion date [   ]

The basis on which I completed my PG/CertEd (FE) was: [   ] Full-time   [   ] Part-time

Below, and on the page opposite are two identical diagrams indication seven key areas in the teaching and supporting of learning in further education. Please think about the extent to which your initial teaching qualification(s) improved your ability in each of these key areas.

Complete Diagram A for CG7306/7   **Complete Diagram B for PG/CertEd (FE)**

If you completed both CG 730 and PG/CertEd (FE) in a two-stage process, please complete both diagrams.

Please insert a number in each box, using the five-point scale where:
1= no improvement at all and 5 = greatly improved, with 2, 3, or 4 indicating positions in between.

Diagram A CG 7306/7

Figure 9.1: continued

Diagram B PG/CertEd (FE)

- Assessing learners' needs
- Reflecting upon & evaluating one's own performance & planning
- Planning & preparing teaching & learning programmes for groups & individuals
- Assessing the outcomes of learning & learners' achievements
- **Teaching and learning in further education**
- Developing & using a range of teaching and learning techniques
- Providing learners with support
- Managing the learning process

Q9 The qualifications I possessed at the time I completed my initial teaching qualification were:
(Please tick all that apply)

☐ General Academic (BA/BSc/BEd)

☐ General Vocational (GNVQ/HNC/HND)

☐ Postgraduate (MA/MSc/MEd/PhD)

☐ Professional Qualifications (please list below)

Q10 In general, how helpful was initial teacher training in improving your ability to teach and support learning?

☐ Not at all helpful   ☐ Quite helpful   ☐ Helpful   ☐ Very helpful

Figure 9.1: continued

For the following questions, please write your answer in the spaces below, or attach a separate sheet of paper if there is insufficient space.

Q11 **What was the <u>most</u> helpful aspect of initial teacher training and why?**

Q12 **What was the <u>least</u> helpful aspect of initial teacher training and why?**

Q13 **If you have taken part in any updating of your initial teacher training, please give details: (what, when, for how long?)**

If you are willing to take part in a short, confidential telephone interview, with an external researcher, about teacher training, please provide the following contact details:

Name   Telephone

e-mail   Best day

                                        and time

Thank you for completing this questionnaire.
Please return it in the envelope provided, to XXXXXXXXXXXXXXXXXXXXXXXXX, by Monday 18 March 2002.

Figure 9.1: continued

If the questionnaire is designed to be read automatically using, for example, a scanner attached to a PC on which is loaded computer software for the analysis of the questionnaire results, completed questionnaires can be quickly coded, scanned and analysed, and a reliable quantitative result obtained. In our example, the questionnaire results were analysed using The Statistical Package for the Social Sciences (SPSS). Themes emerging from this analysis were identified by the research team as a basis for a follow-up interview schedule.

The self-completed questionnaire method can be used in conjunction with other data collection methods, such as interviews, focus group discussions, observations and tests. Questions can be designed to gain confirmation about, or explore more deeply, research issues that have already been raised, for example, in interviews with learners, or in previous reports on the subject.

In her own individual way, Hildi could perhaps call together some peer group researchers from her PGCE course who could help her analyse and identify themes from her questionnaires. She could then carry out interviews to question identified respondents further on these themes.

On-line or other electronic methods of devising questionnaires can also be constructed to be used in a 'live' classroom, seminar or studio situation in which responses to questions from the audience are obtained within seconds, informing the teaching/lecturing situation instantly. Hildi would probably need to get some technical help to set up such a facility, or might need to hire a special venue to carry out her data collection session, but having done so, might find this an exciting and useful method of carrying out research that can influence her teaching situation, though it would need careful design and preparation.

The use of multiple sources of data alongside questionnaires in a small survey is generally recommended, as for example in *case study*, to increase the reliability of the research. Hildi would therefore be wise to consider using questionnaires in conjunction with another form of data collection, to ensure her research is well-grounded and accurate. The survey, as a *research strategy*, may not always reveal accurate answers, as respondents may be bored, tired, filling in answers out of obligation or politeness, and for a multiplicity of their own reasons, may not give trustworthy responses.

Disadvantages – why questionnaires might not be the best or only method

One reason for considering the use of another data collection method alongside or instead of questionnaires, and a hybrid research strategy rather than just the use of a survey strategy using questionnaires, is that there may be the above kinds of potential problems with the accuracy of learners' responses that Hildi should consider. The content of questionnaires in a survey can be misunderstood by learners if they interpret questions in ways the designer had not intended. Responses can also be distorted if learners are unfamiliar with the way questions are presented. Learners sometimes answer questions inaccurately if they have misread or misunderstood the layout or the content of the questions.

The *first major disadvantage* of survey questionnaires, therefore, is that they are very difficult to design in a way that avoids problems of interpretation and presentation. These factors can also relate directly to potential key attributes of the population group to be studied – for example, learners from a minority culture may interpret questions in ways that differ from other groups, or learners with lower levels of educational attainment might have reading problems. This is especially problematic when respondents are from multiple cultural or linguistic backgrounds, or have health, perceptual or other educational problems that can affect understanding. These problems may be so acute – and also so intrinsic to the research – that the researcher might need to rule out the use of questionnaires with a particular population groups, and select other more appropriate data collection methods.

A trial run of the questionnaire process in the form of a *pilot questionnaire*, perhaps based on interviews with learners and also with staff groups who know them, can be helpful to test whether learners are in general likely to understand the kind of language and presentation to be used in the questionnaire, and whether the questionnaire process is in fact a useful method or not. The results of the pilot can then be discussed with learners or other relevant people in a follow-up live interview or group situation, to determine whether the responses that have been given in the pilot accurately reflect learners' real views. Open-ended discussions about the responses – and a self-critical approach with an openness to changes in the draft – can be helpful in this.

The *second major disadvantage* of questionnaires in a survey is that learners' responses may not reflect their real views. They may answer questions to try and please the researcher, or in other ways, perhaps unintentional, may bias their answers to influence perceptions so their behaviour is perceived more positively. Learners may be frightened that the questionnaire process is in fact a test that will reflect poorly on their abilities, and therefore they may attempt to gain falsely positive results. An awareness and avoidance of this kind of learner bias in favour of socially desirable results is necessary in the design process, so that the questionnaires achieve as accurate a result as possible.

Learners may also trivialise responses if they aren't serious about the questionnaire process, and hand in questionnaire results wholly or partly inaccurate or nonsensical. This may be hard to detect, but the researcher needs to be aware of the potential for this, and build into the design process some kind of appropriate way of testing whether results are 'real' or not. Obvious signs of false data would include situations in which respondents give a ridiculous name in their response like 'Micky Mouse', or clearly ignore instructions and fill in inappropriate information. Less obvious methods of spoiling questionnaires may be harder to detect, however. The risk of the potential for this – which is partly dependent on the population group to be researched – is a consideration to be borne in mind in the research design. Surveys are not particularly helpful for deeper exploratory probing of complex issues.

A *third major disadvantage* of the selection of questionnaires as a data collection method, and a survey as the research strategy, is that they usually have fairly low response rates. This can be particularly problematic if the researcher does not know the characteristics of the respondents. In this situation, the researcher cannot easily judge if the sample of respondents who have replied is representative of the general population group to be studied or not.

An example of the need for caution in this might be a whole-college anonymous learner survey of the effectiveness of the canteen service, using questionnaires left in the canteen. If for some reason there was a small group of people who wanted to bias the survey results to their own ends, it might be possible for them to lobby a section of the college population to answer the questions in one particular way, or for one person to fill in multiple questionnaires. If the questionnaires were left unattended, it could be the case that some of them could be tampered with, results changed, or forms taken away and destroyed.

The need for security precautions in such a situation, or perhaps supervision of the data collection process might be necessary, and should be considered in the design of the questionnaires. Awareness and avoidance of the problem of bias arising from security measures or supervision of the process should also be considered, as learners may not fill in a true response on the canteen if the supervisor is, for example, closely watching them complete it!

Designing questionnaires as part of a research strategy

To address these and related problems, very careful design of questionnaires as part of the overall research strategy needs to be carried out. This needs to consider the process of distribution, collection and analysis. In the questionnaire design process, it is useful to draw up an initial draft and circulate this to key informants, who can advise on design and usage. A pilot using the revised draft can then be carried out, the results analysed, and key informants consulted again on the effectiveness of the pilot. Adequate time and resources for this process should be built into the research plan, as it is important to be realistic about the achievability of the questionnaire process, including time for design, redrafting, piloting, final design and printing, distribution, collection, analysis and writing up of results.

Supplementary methods to collect data that can add to the reliability of the questionnaire results include live interviews, telephone surveys or observations. For example, if data were collected on the subject of the retention of refugee or traveller students on FE college courses, a questionnaire alone might be insufficient to reach some students – often from the most vulnerable groups – in a shifting population also characterised by linguistic diversity.

Realism about the likely take-up and success of selecting questionnaires as a data collection method need to be built into the design process – for example, there is not much point in distributing questionnaires to students who can't understand the language used in them or can't read, nor in circulating questionnaires on retention to students who are not there!

Key issues in questionnaire design
Informed consent and right to withdraw

As stated in chapter 7, questionnaire respondents such as Hildi's students need to be asked to give their informed consent to the process of completing a questionnaire.

Fairness and sensitivity

Hildi also needs to be fair and sensitive about the kinds of questions she asks her respondents, and the level of detail and conscientiousness she expects from them. If, for example, her questionnaire is very long and takes considerable time to complete, she needs to consider how fair this is for her learner population, in the context of other demands on their time, and the situation in question. It would not be fair, for instance, for her to give the questionnaire out just before a lunch break in class and to expect her students to stay to complete this and therefore miss their lunch. It would also be insensitive to learners if she handed out a questionnaire about a matter that they would be embarrassed about, in a way in which they were also pressurised to complete it. Even if Hildi had explained to learners previously that they had a right to withdraw, they might be too embarrassed to do so, and might feel threatened and under pressure to answer questions relating to personally sensitive issues that they would rather not address in this public way. Hildi therefore needs to reflect on the potential impact of her questionnaire in terms of the effect that it will have on students.

Guarantee of anonymity or confidentiality

Hildi also needs to give her students a guarantee of confidentiality or anonymity, as appropriate to the group in question and the research process being designed.

Duty to plan for reliability, validity and accuracy in research

It would be both ineffective and unethical if Hildi did not plan for her research findings to be reliable, valid and accurate, when designing her questionnaires. If Hildi was not rigorous about checking the accuracy of her questionnaire, perhaps by making a simple mistake when typing up questions and this mistake was not picked up, learners might be confused by the question, but, regarding it as intentional, might faithfully answer this.

If Hildi's coding and reporting system was based on the original question and not the mistaken one, and if she did not pick up problems when interpreting results, she might report an entirely different answer from the real situation. There is therefore a need not only to plan for a generally high level of reliability and validity, but also rigorously to check the accuracy of questionnaires in terms of design, analysis and reporting.

Purpose and objectives of the questionnaire

Hildi needs to work out what, overall, her questionnaire is going to find out. She needs to be clear about exactly what she wants to find out in the research project. This overall aim then needs to be translated into a set of objectives, from which she can design a series of questions to arrive at conclusions useful to this purpose. For example, if Hildi's overall purpose is to find out whether encouraging students to use individual learning journals in their classroom work is a helpful teaching method, she needs to work out a series of detailed processes and objectives to specify what kind of journal usage will be involved.

Openness to unforeseen results

Hildi also needs to be open to the fact that the research findings may not be at all what she expected. This is in fact one of the main aims of carrying out research in fact – to test the assumptions we readily make, and to question their validity. Hildi's research might discover that the use of learning journals is not helping her students at all. She needs to be open to her own potential bias. One of the key things to assist her in this process is to ensure that her research design is rigorous and well-planned.

Planning the questions

The questionnaire needs to have a clear and logical path of well-structured questions to attract appropriate responses. Hildi should map out her questions so that they logically follow one another. She perhaps might move from general to particular issues, depending on the nature of the research question she is asking overall.

If, for example, in her questionnaire about student satisfaction, she wants to find out whether students enjoy and learn from their lessons, she might find out about their attitude to learning in general first, and their overall feelings about the campus as a learning environment, before moving on to the detail of their lessons. She will then be able to place the respondents' answers in a context that more accurately relates to the overall situation of the learners in the college campus, and this context is likely to be very helpful for the interpretation of her results.

She may find out, for instance, that a major factor in the daytime is disrupting students' satisfaction levels (for example, if building work is being carried out on site), but that this does not interfere with lessons at twilight and in the evenings. Unforeseen responses and new elements will be part of the process of 'finding out': she needs to ensure she does not block these out by focusing questions too narrowly to pick up unexpected responses. This practical consequence derives from the overall approach researchers need to develop in terms of being 'open' to unforeseen results.

Audience for questions – who, how, what, when and where?

Hildi needs to consider in specific detail the audience for her questions. Some basic issues she needs to tackle are the following:

* who will answer the questions?
* how will she ask the questions?
* what kind of questions will she ask?
* when and where will she ask the questions?

The 'who' is the group of respondents that Hildi will be addressing, in this case, her learners. She will need to work out in what ways the sample of responses that she gets will be representative of the whole population – this is not necessarily an easy task. If, for example, all the students in her class from a particular group – say, all those over the age of 30 – either happen to be out that day, or refuse to participate, she may have a problem as regards the accuracy of representation of the responses. She needs to consider this kind of issue when planning the research process.

As regards the 'how' of asking questions, Hildi could plan to print a self-completed questionnaire that she distributes in her class, for completion by students at home , to be returned in an envelope to her. As regards the 'what', or content of the questions, this needs to be tied into her research objectives closely, and the kind of style and language that she uses in asking questions needs to be closely related to the audience's capabilities and characteristics. She also needs to relate the content of the questions to the data analysis methods to be used. For example, if she has decided to use a combination of questions with *preset alternatives* as answers that respondents select using a tick-box system, together with some open questions, Hildi needs to think through in advance how she will analyse the data. The analysis of the preset alternative answers will be much more straightforward than that of the open questions, in which respondents' answers will need to be coded and classified into categories for analysis.

Examples of kinds of questions
Closed questions
Closed questions are fairly easy to code and analyse, and include Yes/No answers, Agree/Disagree answers, choosing from a series of options (a,b,c,d,e), ranking items in a weighted order (give each option a number from 1-10 in order of preference), or ranking items in a pre-set scale such as a Lickert scale (1-5 from 'strongly agree' to 'strongly disagree').

Open questions
By contrast with closed questions, open questions invite respondents to use their own initiative in their answers, as we noted in chapter 8. A combination of methods can be helpful here. Combining a few open questions with some closed questions based on prior interviews with students can enable the researcher to arrive at a workable balance of data collection methods.

1. Do you enjoy your lessons in college? Yes/No
2. Do you think A.N. Other College has good support for learners? Agree/Disagree
3. Which areas of college life are currently most helpful in supporti ng you enjoy and benefit from your studies? Please rate the following responses on a scale of 1 to 5, where '1' means 'most effective' and '5' means 'least effective':

a.	admissions and recruitment	1	2	3	4	5
b.	the learning centre	1	2	3	4	5
c.	the cante en service	1	2	3	4	5
d.	the teachers in my classes	1	2	3	4	5
e.	IT technical support staff	1	2	3	4	5
f.	my personal tutor	1	2	3	4	5

4. Please rate the following responses on a scale of 1 to 5, where '1' means 'strongly agree' and '5' means 'strongly disagree':

a.	I enjoy my lessons in college	1	2	3	4	5
b.	I find my teachers helpful	1	2	3	4	5
c.	My personal tutor is helpful	1	2	3	4	5
d.	Careers staff are supportive	1	2	3	4	5
e.	The admissions staff are good	1	2	3	4	5

Figure 9.2: Example learner support questionnaire – closed questions

1. What aspects of college life do you enjoy the most?
   ....
   ....

2. What aspects of college life do you enjoy the least?
   ....
   ....

3. In what ways do you think the college could support learners more?
   ....
   ....

4. Which class or module have you enjoyed the most this year?
   ....
   ....

5. For what reasons has this been your preferred class or module?
   ....
   ....

Figure9.3: Example learner support questionnaire – open questions

Coding

In designing her questionnaire, Hildi needs to pre-code it, to allow her to classify responses into pre-given categories. Her questionnaire design should include a box for coding responses (usually on the right hand side of the paper). This will make the questionnaire much easier to analyse quickly. In the design of her pilot, she should carry out coding, analysis and reporting of results to ensure all aspects of the questionnaire design work. If she has the resources to link her questionnaire design into an automatic electronic scanner that 'reads' the data and assigns numerical results for closed questions, this will be an inefficient and time-saving method of analysis.

Analysis and results

The analysis of the questionnaires and reporting of results needs to be tied back into the overall aim of the research and the questions initially asked. Statistical analysis is covered in some detail in the next chapter, and in section four we discuss how to write up results in the form of reports and presentations to make use of our research.

Finding out more

Cohen, L:, Manion, L., and Morrison,K., (2000) *Research Methods in Education* (5th edn) London: Routledge

Robson, C. (1993) *Real World Research: A Resource for Social Scientists and Practitioner-Researchers* Oxford: Blackwell Publishers Ltd.

Scholfield, P. (1995) *Quantifying Language: A Researcher's and Teacher's Guide to Gathering Language Data and Reducing it to Figures* Clevedon: Multilingual Matters Ltd. (very useful detailed examination of language issues in data collection and the quantification of these)

10
Working with statistics

Barry has a headache. He has been sitting in front of his computer for most of the day, searching through spreadsheets and inputting information about learners' achievements. He has to complete this work by the end of the week, to ensure that the information is ready for the Adult Learning Inspectorate (ALI) inspection taking place next month. His principal goal is to ensure that the inspectors will have the most up to date information possible about how the institution has been recruiting learners and enabling them to gain qualifications and achieve their learning goals.

The difficulty that Barry faces is that he is not quite sure what particular data the inspectors may ask for. He has an enormous amount of information stored in various spreadsheets and databases. He has information on the numbers of people applying for each programme of study offered in the college. He has information relating to the previous qualifications of all learners enrolled on programmes of study from the past ten years, although he knows that some of this information is not fully accurate or complete. He has information stored on all previous learners and their achievements going back ten years. He has information of how many learners completed their programmes of study. He even knows where they all live and if their postcode defines them as being in the category of 'widening participation' learners.

The data held about learners in his college can be compared with national benchmarks and statistics. The local press is bound to be interested in how the college fares against other regional and national institutions. How can Barry make appropriate use of the information he has been collating over the years, and how can it help other colleagues make sensible decisions about recruiting and retaining learners so that they can achieve their learning goals?

Many people find that anything to do with numbers will result in feelings of panic, insecurity or downright boredom. Yet throughout policies in post-compulsory education, 'facts and figures' are quoted relentlessly. Target figures are created, such as the 50% participation rate for people under 30 in higher education by the year 2010. Achievement rates in A levels are written in rank order by the national and educational press. Individual subject areas have benchmarks of national rates of achievement against which individual institutions can measure themselves. Every year, in August, when GCSE and A Level results are announced, there are cries of 'dumbing down' and 'falling standards'. How can practitioners analyse such figures and also have sufficient understanding of their provenance to make judgements about what they actually mean?

Counting and making it count

The simplest way to examine how often or how much a phenomenon occurs is to count it. If we want to know how popular a particular programme area is, we could add up the number of people studying it. With all measures, this is not accurate enough because there are so many other factors that may limit this phenomenon under examination. Our most popular subject may appear so because we have more capacity in this programme area, compared to one which has more demand but fewer places available. With any measurement, then, we must take care that we are using an appropriate way of 'counting' and that we are aware of the factors that contribute to the thing we are measuring. Once we have counted our phenomena, we can begin to express it in different ways.

Numbers can mean different things

If we consider the example above, where Barry is dealing with student achievement, then we may be looking at numbers of students, their grades, and how long they took to gain these qualifications. We may also have information about their previous qualifications. Data are *discrete* or *continuous*. *Nominal* data are discrete – people are either male or female. *Continuous* data are those which stretch along a continuum, such as height and weight. Some of the information that Barry is examining is nominal, because it relates to a characteristic which people possess or not: male or female, taking an A level or an NVQ. There is no sliding scale for that kind of data. However, if we have information about their test results, then the information may be grouped, so that there are grades. For example, a pass may be given to an examination mark over 40, with an A grade for a mark over 70. This kind of information can be placed in what is known as *rank order*, in other words, we can line up our group of learners and put them in order of the highest mark down to the lowest mark. We could, if we wanted to, try to find out the learner with the highest mark in the college. However, we may find this difficult if we have different types of mark and grading. An NVQ is either pass or fail, whereas with A levels, we have grades A to E. In a simple class test, we may have scores ranging from 1-100, which are continuous. So you can see that already we have a problem with some of our data, in that we cannot easily compare like with like. Yet we may be asked to demonstrate that our rate of achievement is healthy across our programme areas.

What *can* we do with our data? Well, one of the most useful questions we can answer is how our learners have fared compared with learners from the same programme in previous years. This can help us know if any changes to our teaching and learning methods have improved the success rate for our learners. We may want to examine if males perform differently from females. We could divide all our data into two groups, and rank order them for males and females. We may find that males perform very well at the highest range of marks, but they also are over represented at the lower end. The females are all clustered in the middle. Yet if we examine our data more carefully, we may find that this is because the type of programmes taken by the males have a marking system of grades, whereas the programmes taken primarily by females is more pass/fail. Again, we must be careful making judgements when we are not comparing like with like.

Once we know what kind of data we have, we can then begin to analyse it. This is where we begin to use statistics.

Descriptive and analytical statistics

When Barry is looking at his spreadsheets, he cannot possibly tell if there are any trends. He could not describe what he has in front of him, as he quite simply cannot look at all the figures at the same time. So he needs a way to capture this information. Then he will be able to analyse it more carefully. Working with figures therefore requires ways to describe the data, and then to analyse them.

Most people are familiar with the notion that numbers can be expressed as parts of a whole, like fractions, percentages and decimals. You will encounter these in many research articles. However, it is important that you understand exactly what is being expressed. A decimal such as 0.426 of 10 people is a bit meaningless, as we can't actually divide a whole person into parts! With that word of caution, let us now explore how we can use the phenomena we have counted to make sense of it.

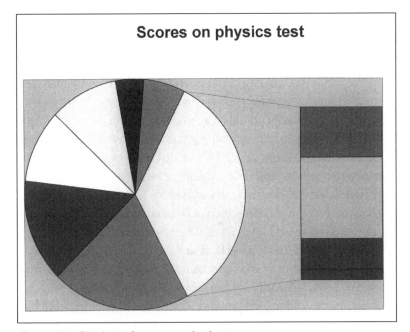

Figure 10.1: Pie chart of scores on physics test

The simplest forms of description occur where frequencies of particular events are calculated. You will have seen many examples of such descriptive statistics on television, when bar charts or pie charts are used. These are visual ways to capture how many people vote a certain way, for example, what percentage do so, in the case of a pie chart. If we look at our A level scores, we can represent these in a bar chart, pie chart or even on a graph.

However, this does not really tell us much. The really helpful aspect of statistics is that we can use them to help us search for links between aspects of the information. Before we do this, we need to think of the type of relationships we are seeking, and what kind of data we have.

When we have a set of results, we may want to know what the average performance is. There is more than one way to express what the average mark is. Let us look at the example below.

Here we have the results from the modules of a Physics A level for two groups of learners. The first thing we need to do is to put the results in rank order. Then we can begin to work out which result occurs most. The name for this kind of average is the *mode*. It means

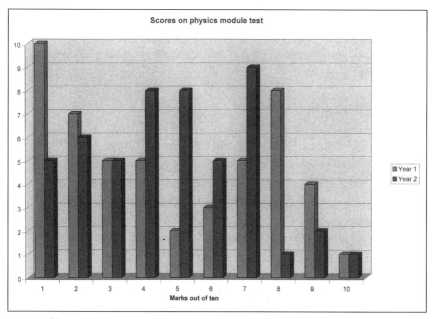

Figure 10.2: Bar chart of scores of physics test

the most frequently occurring number. For group one, the mode is the score of one, whereas for group two, the mode is the score seven.

However, this may not be what we want. So perhaps we want to know what the half way mark is, which is another way of expressing the average score. Having put our results in rank order, we can now find the half way mark and this score is now our *median*. For group one, the median is between four and five, so we simply halve it and say it is 4.5.For group two it is five

However, if we look at our results, we do seem to have a lot of results at both ends, that is, many people gained high results or low results. The other way of calculating the average is to add up all the scores, divide them by the number of people gaining those scores, and the answer is the arithmetic *mean*. For group one, the mean is 4.36, and for group 2 it is 5.92. With this calculation, we see that our average mark has been dragged down towards a lower grade in group one because of the polarised nature of the results for the group. You may now begin to see why it is very important to know what kind of average is being talked about in reports in the national press. If we wanted to show that our average mark is a good one, we may decide to use the mode for group two. If we want to show that results are getting worse, we may use the mean. All of these averages, mean, median and mode are perfectly acceptable mathematical analyses of our data. Our *interpretation* of our data depends on which calculation we choose to use.

Normal distribution

What is an average measure? Many of you may be frustrated when shopping for clothes, because there are standard sizes based on 'average' measurements. If we asked the population of England to line up in order of their height, we would find that there are a large number of people who are between 150-170 cms , but far fewer who are less than 140 cms or over 190 cms tall. We can show this distribution on what is called a *bell curve*, or *gaussian curve*. In any population, for any measure such as height, weight, shoe size, we will find that there are more people in the middle measurements, and fewer at either end. We say that a normal distribution occurs when the frequency of occurrences for the mid point of any measure is at its highest, and the frequency on either side diminishes.

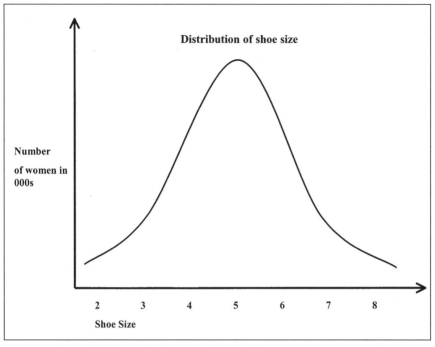

Figure 10.3: Example of a normal distribution

Now, the shape of the curve can differ quite a bit. Where we have quite a split between scores, such as in our example with physics results, then the mean, median and mode are not only different, the shape of the distribution curve also changes. One of the more controversial measurements we can make is of people's intelligence. A person's IQ score (intelligence quotient) is based on the idea that the 'average' score is 100, and that half the population has a score higher than this, and half below. Now, if we look at small sections of the whole population, we may find that they are over or under represented along the full range of scores. A great deal of controversy has arisen since IQ scores were first gained from IQ tests, because these scores could be examined in terms of a person's racial background, class background or religion. This has led some psychologists and politicians to claim that certain groups have genetically lower intelligence than others. This is another area where statistics can be used to support ideological ideas. The difficulty is that IQ scores represent a person's performance on a particular test which may have cultural bias built in, and does not represent a person's 'intelligence' as such. However, if we return to our example of learners' test results, we can see that we may have a distribution that is 'normal', or one that is skewed. It would be possible to develop a series of profiles of different results from different types of programme, and we may find that over time, these do not change much. In other words, we may find that certain programmes attract learners who perform highly, and other programmes where they perform badly. We can them begin to examine what we *do* about this information.

Standard Deviation

Another important statistic that we should examine when we look at the distribution of any measure is to see how spread out the results are. Our distribution of scores could all be very close together, in which case our curve would be very tall and thin. If our scores are very spread out along the range of possible values, then our curve will be very wide. It helps to know about the spread of scores, because the larger the spread, the less useful the mean becomes. As our earlier example showed, if there are many scores at either end of the range, our mean gives us a false idea that most people gained scores in the middle of the range. The measure that we use to tell us about the spread is called standard deviation. Here, we look at the difference between any individual's score and the mean. We calculate the standard deviation by adding up all these differences, but we square them first, because people who have scored less than the mean would have a negative score, and this would present us with a different result. We then divide the sum of the squares by the number of people or cases that we have. Standard deviation is used in tandem with the mean, so that we can understand what kind of spread we have in the data. Figure 9.4 shows a typical bell curve with the standard deviations showing. As you can see, the first standard deviation is fairly close to the mean, and the second is much further apart.

Sampling

An important use of numerical information is where we use it to help us choose which groups of people or things we wish to investigate in the first place. This process is known as sampling.

You may have read in papers about percentages of people who have a particular characteristic, or behaviour. Polls of voting behaviour are an example of this. About 1000 people may have been asked to

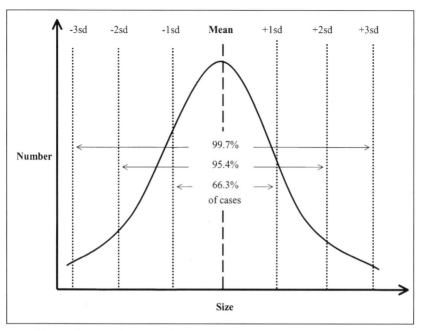

Figure 10.4: standard deviation

state which political party they are intending to vote for. This preference is then measured over the weeks prior to a government election. Trends show one political party becoming more or less favoured than another. Now, choosing the sample of people is very important to reflect the nature of the country as a whole (although we also know that different groups of people vote more than others, 'skewing' the results of any election to be non-representative of the total population of the country). The way in which people are chosen arises from a sampling strategy.

There are different types of sampling. If you stand outside the college canteen at lunchtime and ask learners what they think about college catering facilities, you may be talking to only one group of people, ie those who buy food and drink. There may be numerous groups of part time learners who only come to the institution in the evenings, and you will not obtain their views at lunchtime. The people in the evenings may all be adults, whereas the daytime people may primarily be young people. You are likely to obtain different responses from these groups. In terms of using statistics, it is important to remember where your data are coming from, and whether your sample does reflect the population as a whole, in this case, learners at your college.

The simplest sample method is the where we take a *random sample*. We firstly need a sampling frame, such as young people aged 14-19 in the college. Now, if we want to ask a group of these young people to complete a questionnaire, for example, our simple sampling method is where we pick at random from the complete list of learners in this sampling frame. Each person has as much chance of being picked as another.

Another way to gain a sample within the sampling frame is to pick people *systematically*, such as every fifth person on the list. Again, this ensures that people have an equal likelihood of being picked, and the researcher is not deliberately biased in the choice of participant.

We can be more deliberate in our choice of people if we take a *stratified sample*. Here, we divide people into groups before we make our choice. The groups, or strata, must have a very clear criterion for being chosen, such as people from different age groups, or subjects being studied. Then we apply our random or systematic sample procedure to obtain our group or sample that we wish to explore. Obviously, it is important to clarify why the groups are divided in this way. There is no point doing so just for the sake of it. However, if we wanted to examine differences in retention rates across different disciplines, then using a stratified sample is an appropriate mechanism.

What happens if we have different numbers of people to choose from within our strata? This will happen, particularly in our example of learners drawn from across different disciplines. One way to deal with this is to take a percentage from each strata, therefore representing the overall population spread. This happens in market research, where people are stratified in terms of social class, sex and age, and then researchers have a target number of people to interview from each category.

If we did not do this, we would end up oversampling from certain groups. Then our data would be biased in favour of these respondents. The whole purpose of sampling is to minimise bias.

When you read about surveys and questionnaires in the press, or in project reports, always check how many people were asked to take part, and how many actually did take part. Often, despite asking the appropriate number within any one strata to participate, there may be differences between the groups in their levels of response. This will also lead to bias in the data analysis phase.

Another important point to remember is about sample size. It is not always necessary to obtain the largest possible sample in your research. On the other hand, it is not acceptable to generalise from a small sample to the whole population. Very often in press reports, scare mongering headlines about results from a survey belies a small sample who contributes to a survey. Thus, a finding that 90% of people do not like the current Prime Minister would not be accurate if you had stood outside the Conservative Club in middle England for your survey! Another important point to remember when capturing data descriptively is on how to express small numbers. It is not sensible to talk about percentages with less than 10 respondents! 5.5% of respondents from a group of seven individuals is meaningless.

Different types of variable

When we try to find out if there are any relationships between our data, we need to think about the nature of this information. Each measure is defined as a variable, quite simply because the measure can actually vary from one example to another. The information pertaining to each variable is called data, and one single piece of information is a datum. So, a variable comprises data taken from each instance of measurement. I have already mentioned that there are different types of variable, nominal (such as sex, religion, family type) and *ordinal* (where we place values in rank from highest to lowest, largest to smallest). There is another type of measurement where we group values together. This is known as an *interval* variable. Suppose we ask our group of learners how many times they study each week. We may find that their responses vary from never, once a week, twice a week up to nine times a week. For the purposes of analysing our data to see if there are any trends, we may find that it is easier to group our responses into three different categories, using intervals of 1-3 times a week, 4-6 times a week and 7-9 times a week. Note that by doing this, any one response now fits exactly into one of our intervals. We may decide to ask our respondents to tick one of these categories, instead of choosing an exact number. This is not because we cannot be bothered with more detail, but because we know enough about human behaviour that people are not always accurate in their reporting, and intervals are more likely to obtain a response which bears some relation to the reality than precise numbers.

Much research talks about qualitative and quantitative data. Qualitative data largely concern nominal variables, because there is no inherent numerical value present. People's views about a new teaching strategy, for example, cannot be expressed numerically until they are asked to give it a value, such as how strongly they feel about the success of the implementation. Then the variable may become ordinal, or even interval.

Statistical tests

Statistical tests are best suited to variables which are at the interval level. This is partly because the tests are based on an assumption that the data are of this kind, and partly because we can convey more information with this kind of data than nominal or ordinal variables. However, our kind of research does not always fit this kind of variable, and we need to be very cautious about using different statistical tests when dealing with information about people which often needs to be examined in terms of nominal and ordinal variables.

The important point to remember when reading about statistics is that data convey information which is then interpreted. Some data are more helpful than others, and generally, there is more information in interval data than in nominal. The statistical tests which pertain to each of these types of variable, therefore, also vary in their power to interpret. There is no statistical test that provides a hundred per cent explanation for any phenomenon. Each test is based on assumptions about the nature of the data and the way in which they can be interpreted.

Now that we have divided how we obtain our data into types of variable, we can begin to identify which statistical tests help us to interpret the results. There are two major types of statistical test, parametric and non-parametric. The former assumes that the data are placed in interval scales, in other words are continuous, and truly can be measured, such as height and weight. The other type of statistical test, non-parametric, makes no such assumption. Generally speaking, the type of test which should be applied to responses to a small-scale questionnaire would be a non-parametric test. It does not assume that the rating of 2 on the scale is equidistant from the numbers 1 and 3. This may seem rather strange, but if you think of how you fill out questionnaires, you often find yourself using the middle score to capture all sorts of thoughts including 'I don't really know' , 'I don't really care' as well as 'I really think it is about half way'. People tend not to use extremes in rating scales, and therefore we cannot assume that these have the same value for them as the middle points in a scale.

At this point, you may be wondering why we make such a fuss about data, how they are measured and how we use statistical tests to interpret them. Well, let us look at the example of A level scores. Not only is measuring examination and coursework performance fraught with difficulty in terms of how accurate these methods of assessment capture someone's understanding of the subject, we introduce further error by aggregating scores and analysing the results into measures of overall performance, and then use this information to make judgements about allotting grades.

Government funding may well follow certain analyses of examination results. If we introduce a new scheme, such as modular examinations, then we really do need to know which statistical test to apply, as our data may not actually behave in the way that the statistical test assumes.

There are numerous books on using statistical methods, and those of you who will need to apply statistical tests to your own data, or who need to interpret those used by others, may like to refer to the recommended reading list at the end of this chapter.

Correlations

The simplest type of statistical calculation we can make for comparing data is to use *correlation*. Here, we line up one set of data against another. Suppose we want to know if attending personal tutorials makes any difference to pass rates for A levels for our 16-19 year old learners. If we had 100 learners, we could create a table of data that has one column which shows how many tutorials they attended, and a second column with their grade results. We then undertake a particular statistical calculation to identify if there is a strong link between the two. We might expect that the more tutorials attended, the higher the grade. In fact, we could imagine a situation where there is a perfect match between the number of tutorials attended and the grade gained. If we plotted the number of tutorials against grades in a graph, a perfect match would look like a straight line at 45^0. Of course, we could have a negative link, the more tutorials attended, the lower the grade, and we could explain this because learners requiring more help may not be coping with the level of study required and need more support. Figure 10.5 shows a correlation with a perfect match between number of tutorials and grade obtained

It is important to remember that correlations are not the same as causes. Just because we find a strong link or strong correlation between two variables does not mean that we can claim that one causes

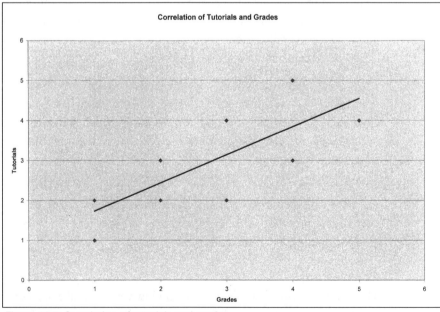

Figure 10.5: Correlation of tutorials and grades

the other. We do not know the direction of influence with a correlation, only that the two variables align themselves to more or less extent. It is better to think of them as two circles from a Venn diagram. Where there is an overlap, there is a correlation. The more overlap, the stronger the correlation. The maximum overlap is where the circles become one. A correlation has a value between -1 and +1. No correlation at all is expressed as 0. There are statistical tests to help us know whether our correlation is significant or not, as it is possible to obtain a strong correlation, particularly with large numbers, when we cannot claim with any confidence that a relationship exists outside that of pure chance.

Choosing statistical tests

When you want to create a measure of a particular phenomenon, then you need to think about what kind of variable you are measuring. Suppose Barry wants to see if there is any significant relationship between the retention figures for groups of learners who were taking a certificate in information technology in the first five years of the period he has data on, compared with the revised NVQ version of this course during the last five years. What kind of data does Barry have?

Firstly, he has demographic data on learner's age, sex, previous qualifications and where they live. Secondly, he has information on their success rate. Finally, he has data on the grades of the certificate, but not of the NVQ.

We now need to know what variable is dependent on what other variable. There are two types of variable, dependent and independent. The *independent* variable exists regardless of what we are interested in measuring, such as age and sex. We want to know if the programme has affected the success rate. So our *dependent* variable is the programme, and how this relates to the success rate. If you are not sure which is which, always ask yourself the question what do I want to know and on what does it depend?

Now that we know which is our dependent variable, we can begin to test out our question. It helps if we make ourselves a hypothesis or hunch. We could say that we think the success rate was better with the old certificate. So our hypothesis would state that the success rate in qualifications in information technology depends on the type of learning programme provided. Non competence based certificates are more successful than NVQs.

We could even create an 'if then' statement, such as if learners take the certificate course, they are more likely to succeed than if they take the NVQ. Now you can imagine that this is a pretty dangerous statement to make within a college trying to gain a high quality rating in its inspection. What is your evidence?

Let's look at table 10.1. As you can see, we have different numbers of people taking the old certificate and the new NVQ. We can't simply just state that more people did not complete the NVQ, as there were more people studying for this qualification than in the old certificate. The actual numbers are not helpful to us in identifying if there is any relationship between the different programmes and the success rate.

	Pass	Fail	Total
Certificate	30	20	50
NVQ	20	30	50
Total	50	50	100

Table10.1: Achievement rates for Certificate and NVQ awards

Chi Square

The type of data we have is nominal, as we have pass and fail for the NVQ and Certificate. We now want to compare two different variables. This means that we have to make a cross tabulation. When we have put our results into the four different cells, as shown below, we now need to know if the results are different from each other due to the type of programme. We therefore need to apply a statistical test. One of the tests we could use is called the Chi Square. This test is non-parametric, which is what we want. It starts from the premise that we could have expected equal results if there were no difference between the groups of learners that we have

We can choose pass/fail and certificate/NVQ as our variables to analyse. As you can see below, we have actual success rates, compared with expected success rates. The Chi Square test is used to see if there is a *significant* difference between our actual results compared with our expected results.

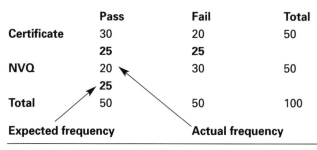

	Pass	Fail	Total
Certificate	30	20	50
	25	**25**	
NVQ	20	30	50
	25		
Total	50	50	100

Expected frequency   Actual frequency

Table 2: Chi Square Calculation for Achievement Rates

Although it is important to know how to calculate a chi square yourself, luckily there are numerous statistical and spreadsheet packages that can do the computation for you. However, you do need to know what you are obtaining from the print out.

Let's introduce some more statistical terms

Degrees of freedom

The simplest way to describe degrees of freedom is to think of the game musical chairs. You walk around a set of chairs, and when the music stops, you have to find somewhere to sit down. Let us assume that it is the first round, and there are enough chairs for everybody and there are ten chairs and ten people. When the music stops, the first person sits down. Now you have only 9 chairs left to chose from. Once the next person sits down, you have only got 8 chairs to chose from. In, the end, when there is only one chair remaining, you have no choice. In a sense, degrees of freedom are like choosing chairs. The last one is never a choice, so you have one less than the total number of options that you start from. In a table such as above, where we have two columns and two rows, our degrees of freedom in each is only one, because we have two possible cells to put our data in, but only one option. If we had three rows, we would have two degrees of freedom. In other words, for any number n, we have n-1 degrees of freedom.

When we have a table, we then multiply the degrees of freedom for the rows by the columns. Again, as it happens, as each row and column has only one degree of freedom, our degrees of freedom for this test is still 1, as 1x1=1.

Significance

A really important term used in statistics is the word *significance*. In everyday language, we use the word significant to mean important, or something to take notice of. In statistics, it has a very special meaning, and it is vital that you do not get the two uses mixed up when talking about results. Statistically, a result is significant if we can state with a high level of confidence that there is a relationship between our variables. Now, we can never be one hundred percent sure that our relationship does exist. We may have data that do not represent what we are measuring (such as IQ tests being a measure of intelligence!). We may have results that have occurred simply by chance. It is often possible to take two separate measures, run a statistical test on them and find that there is a relationship in the data that does not actually mean anything. You could, for example, try to find out if eating muesli for breakfast is related to shoe size. You cannot say that eating muesli causes changes to shoe size, or even that having a certain shoe size makes you eat muesli. It is just sheer chance that the two happen to be related.

We can therefore make different types of error about our analysis of our data

Type one error is where we say there is a relationship when it does not exist, and type two is where we say there is no relationship when there is.

As you may now be increasingly aware, statistics is all about making assumptions, and making errors! The use of tests, particularly where significance is concerned, is to try to minimise the possibility of getting the results 'wrong', either way. The best way to treat statistical tests is with a great deal of caution.

Each statistical test has a test for significance. As noted above, this is to help us decide whether we do have a relationship that is not a result of sheer chance. In general, the larger the number of people or cases in a sample, the more likelihood of finding a relationship that exists.

One term that you will read in the research literature is about rejecting the null hypothesis. This basically means that a null hypothesis, which states that there is no relationship, has to be rejected because the evidence from the data and the statistical analysis is that there *is* a relationship. You will also see that the rejection of the null hypothesis is usually accompanied by a figure, such as 0.05 level. This means that our result is likely to show a relationship if we repeated our research 95% of the time. The 5% is a small chance that we got it wrong, and it was sheer fluke that our results came out this way. The best way to think of this is to imagine tossing a coin one hundred times. The result will always be heads or tails, but we could have a coin that is slightly weighted resulting in heads falling more than tails. If the coin is perfectly balanced, it would still be possible to throw one hundred tails, but is far more unlikely.

The power of a statistical test is in its ability to show that a relationship exists when it really does. However, the level of significance is all to do with the probability that the relationship arises by chance. If you see that something is reported to be significant at the 0.05 level, and another result significant at the 0.001 level, this does not mean that the relationship between the variables is stronger in the second case, only that the first case is more probable than the latter of arising by chance.

Finally

The world of statistics can seem both daunting and meaningless. The best way to approach this is to think about the kind of data being used, and to remember that the point of statistics is to help describe data and help us infer some relationship between the variables. If you read any research literature which includes statistics, remember to ask yourself if the data and its interpretation has been appropriately analysed with the statistical tests reported. Ask yourself if the numbers involved justify the interpretation and conclusion. If you can do this, you are already operating at a level of critique which will enable you to make sensible judgements about the research.

Finding out more

There are numerous texts on using statistics. Some of these are more technical than others. As a starting point, we recommend

Bryman, A., and Cramer, D. (1990) *Quantitative Data Analysis for Social Scientists* London: Routledge

Cohen, L:, Manion, L., and Morrison, K. (2000) *Research Methods in Education* (5th edn) London: Routledge

De Vaus, D. (2002) *Analyzing Social Science Data: 50 Key Problems in Data Analysis* London: Sage

Section Four
Making use of research and going further

Chapter 11
Making use of research

Making use of research effectively is critically important for the FE sector. In December, 2002, the then Minister for Lifelong Learning and Higher Education, Margaret Hodge, reinforced this point at the Learning and Skills Research Network annual conference, saying,

> 'We are passionate about improving learners' outcomes and widening participation. The role of research is very important and the work you are doing is now centre stage. But often the research arrives too late and the policy has already moved on.'
> (Hodge, 2002)

The FE sector needs to address the usefulness, and timeliness of practitioner research, making sure that it is closely linked to learning outcomes for students and college goals overall. This in turn needs to influence policy driving the sector.

The strenuous attempts of the Learning and Skills Development Agency to create over a number of years a new paradigm for research in the national Learning and Skills Research Network as a useful, practical, evidence-based educational activity have therefore faced resistance in this long-term view of research as 'inappropriate' for FE.

Examples of existing local research that have generally been readily accepted for their direct effectiveness are in areas such as market research, management information systems analysis, student surveys, staff development information and analysis, information and communications technology, geodemographic postcode analysis for widening participation, destinations analysis and retention/ achievement data analysis. Many FE practitioners are constantly carrying out such local analyses to provide information for practical day-to-day tasks and projects in colleges, and routinely regarding this as part of their work. For example, the IT manager will often regularly monitor the use of college software programmes, reporting on this to college management using statistical analysis and qualitative feedback from local questionnaires to make a case for new purchases.

These kinds of research projects often produce 'hard' quantifiable data and findings that have been used in FE for a variety of immediately practical purposes, from introducing new management information systems to attracting new client groups to study at the college. This kind of 'useful' data and analysis is readily accepted as a norm of good practice in further education, particularly in relation to such activities as preparation for inspection and the introduction of new managerial, marketing, ILT, canteen, nursery, MIS, security or admissions systems changes. Yet, ironically, this kind of activity is sometimes not recognised as 'research' at all!

Using and implementing the results of our own research
Many staff in FE also regularly complete more formal research projects for dissertations, theses and other projects for higher degrees and advanced diplomas relating to their subject areas. These are usually reports of small local research studies, written for the specific purpose of obtaining a qualification. Few of these small-scale research projects have been sufficiently recognised and celebrated. We speculate that perhaps even fewer research projects are used by practitioners to develop and improve work in our own colleges.

To recognise our own voice as practitioners in research we need to:

• put aside the myth that research is 'only for higher education and industry'

• keep up to date with the development of new knowledge and practice

- analyse and value the authenticity of original practitioner research

- use 'critical friends' in practitioner networks to improve and develop our work

- increase confidence by analysing our work with rigour and discernment

- identify barriers to the implementation of our own research

- draw up an implementation strategy to overcome these barriers

Put aside the myth that research is 'only for higher education and industry'

Often the results of large national research projects are very useful, and practitioners doing small-scale research work could never compete in terms of scale and expertise. This does not, however, mean that we should undervalue the work carried out by everyday practitioners in classrooms, libraries and college business and management offices. It is more a question of a difference in scale of funding and level of expertise.

Keep up to date with the development of new knowledge and practice

Practitioners carrying out research projects may find continuous professional development, including industrial placement, a particularly useful way of ensuring we are kept informed of new ideas in our expert field. Another useful method of professional updating is to ensure that we attend research network or other subject specific meetings of practitioners or join in conference presentations and research dissemination activities.

Analysing the results of our research

Updating our field of knowledge is one way to ensure we develop the skills to carry out an analysis of the usefulness of our research. We can also work with peer researchers to develop 'critical friends' who can support us in a critique of our own work. Working with an action research group for collaborative planning and supervision of the overall research project enables us to establish a sense of objectivity.

Through this action research group, effective analysis of the results of our research can be developed in partnership. A supervisory research group will have a function partly to support objective analytical guardianship of the research project. This applies particularly if the research project is publicly funded. It is therefore important that we apply formal procedures to ensure analytical objectivity of our research and the findings it has enabled. Having a formally appointed supervisor, critical friend or mentor can also be a useful strategy to enable us to talk through the results of analysis of the research process, data collection and analysis of findings.

Value the authenticity of original practitioner research

To some FE practitioners, everyone else is an authority except them. Quoting from books by others, we sometimes vest in others the power and authority we are frightened to assume ourselves. It is time for practitioners to learn to value our own authenticity, and the value of our own reflections and the research that stems from that. Growth in confidence comes from recognising the value that practitioners' own ideas and work can bring.

Use critical friends and practitioner networks to improve our work

The concept of a 'critical friend' is particularly useful for practitioners in further education, who may have little support and help to carry out research projects. It is recommended that for our research project we should find a 'critical friend' to help us, preferably a peer group member, with similar interests to our own, with whom we can develop mutual friendly critical feedback on research projects. Collaborative practitioner networks usually provide many opportunities to develop relationships with peer group members working on similar projects to our own.

Increase confidence by analysing our work with rigour and discernment

There is considerable benefit from an open and friendly recognition that more discipline and rigour is needed to improve our research. Having faced this, we can obtain help from practitioner networks of researchers providing support in research methodology: using this knowledge and improved technique will in turn increase our confidence to carry out research effectively.

Identify barriers to the implementation of our own research

In further education, teachers, administrative workers, managers and other professionals are often faced with multiple competing ongoing tasks, with little time even to reflect, let alone carry out research projects and implement them. If time and resource issues are the main barrier to implementation of our research, there are possibilities for these barriers to be overcome.

Draw up an implementation strategy to overcome barriers

Having openly recognised the barriers to implementation of our research, we then need to work out a way to overcome these. It may be helpful to draw up an implementation strategy for our research.

This should consist of an action plan and targets specifying any resources and additional time we need to implement research. We might then approach management with a proposal to implement our research, bidding for realistic funds for the project. We could also use this action plan for a funding bid to the LSDA, local LSC or other interested body such as a university advertising FE fellowships, for external funds to help us implement existing research findings and take our projects further.

As we have raised many times in this book, FE is generally an extremely 'difficult' sector in which to obtain the funds and the time to carry out research. It may be the case, therefore, that it will be difficult to implement our own research findings fully and effectively unless we proactively outline a strategy to implement research through external funding, and carry this through effectively.

However, there are other possibilities for effective implementation. These include using our existing resources within the classroom or workplace to carry forward the results of some of our findings. For example, if we have discovered that a particular method of teaching always works best to teach certain concepts, we can decide to implement this in our own lessons in a planned and monitored way, and report the results to our departmental group, or make a presentation to a conference. We can carry these kinds of activities out with minimal expenditure in a realistic way.

A basic strategy for the implementation of practitioner research findings

- identify any links between our research and national, regional and local policy

- work out key messages from our research findings

- identify the differences between current practice(s) and our research findings

- decide which practice(s) need to be changed

- identify barriers to changing practice(s) and the means to overcome them

- work out methods to implement the changes in practice(s) identified

- implement the methods in pilot studies

- monitor, evaluate, report disseminate the results of pilot

- feedback into the policy-making process

- work out the key messages and implement pilot findings

- undertake further research and implement results

The above snapshot gives a basic strategy for implementing practitioner research findings, and feeding these upwards into policy formation at a local, and hopefully regional or national level. This is a spiral process which should ideally be continuous, leading to improved quality.

Writing up research reports

Best practice guidelines are provided by Gough (2000) and Orna and Stevens (1995) to write up research reports. We have also previously (Jameson and Hillier, 2003) provided such a guide for post compulsory education research reports. Such guides suggest we should from the outset organise all our information to fit into the structure we will use in the final report, by categorising information into

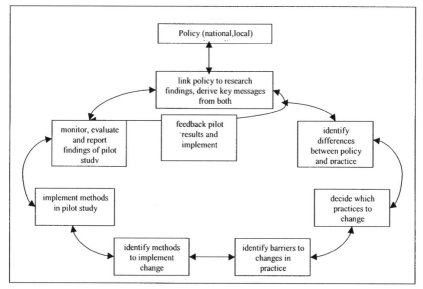

Figure 11.1: Strategy for implementing FE practitioner research findings linked to policy

sections. The following simple guide to help plan our report may help us if we follow it:

1. Draw up a logical list of categories for our final report, such as:

   - contents
   - introduction
   - background
   - methodology
   - data collection
   - analysis
   - findings
   - conclusion
   - references

Write a contents list of chapters for the report based on these categories as illustrated in Figure 11.2 Then break these sections down into subsections, for example: Background: Sections 1, 2, 3, as illustrated in Figure 11.3:

- place markers for all information for report into subsections

- mark out key ideas throughout report within subsections

CONTENTS

introduction	setting for research, making case, research question to be explored, reasons for research
background	current educational trends, nature of subject area, local issues, background provided by literature on the subject
methodology	explanation of strategy and methods
data collection	description of data collected: nature of collection methods carried out
analysis	report of data analysis: statistical, quantitative or qualitative analysis, triangulation methods
findings	discussion of research findings from analysis
conclusions	conclusions drawn, pointers to further work
references	full list of references cited in the report

Figure 11.2: Contents

- group ideas together into themes, write up separate list of themes, number these

- in list of contents, install numbered themes in appropriate ways under each chapter

- divide list of contents with themes into boxes with extra space and print out.

- in the print-out of boxes containing information, write out fully draft sections

- compile the final framework for report and start writing.

Dissemination

Widespread dissemination is necessary for wide readership and ownership of the research report. It is helpful to arrange for the draft report to be circulated widely to invite comments in a realistic time-

Contents of report

1. introduction

- description of setting for college
- previous studies summarized
- nature of student group
- retention issues
- issues to be explored

describe setting for research and for college, nature of subject to be researched, reason for research, summary of previous research studies, description of student group, issues to be explored and investigated.

2. current educational trends

- nature of subject area
- local data

current educational trends, nature of subject area, local data from index of deprivation, local jobs available in area of work.

3. background

- local situation in more detail

further detail on background to local research situation and reasons for investigation

4. methodology described

- research strategy
- methods to be used

strategy and methods in detail: for example a hybrid strategy involving multiple case study, multiple sources of evidence

5. data collection

- description of method
- reporting of process

description of data collection process and detailed reports on data collected

6. case studies (if appropriate)

- detailed in-depth individual case studies

several in-depth case studies describing typical individual in detail

7. analysis

- description of data analysis
- reporting of results of data analysis

reporting results: detailed analytical process, triangulation of results, depth of issues

8. findings

reporting overall findings

9. conclusion

conclusions summarising key issues

suggested further research

Figure 11.3: Suggested draft of subsections within chapters against contents list for report

scale. We can then circulate copies of the comments received, and let everyone know the report will be revised. If, however, there are important sensitivities surrounding this wide distribution owing to the nature of the data collected or the nature of the report, we may need to be a bit more circumspect about circulation of the draft to key participants first. This may include any identified person who is likely to have ownership or sensitivity about the report and the nature of the research carried out.

It is really worth observing these processes of shared public dissemination and ownership to ensure that the report is, in the long run, well received in the community in which the research took place. Having observed ethnical and political sensitivities, generally an open, wide dissemination of the report in a democratic way is an appropriate style of communication for the results of action research, as it is keenly rooted in the ownership of the group

Having reflected on the way to make use of our research findings in practice, we now examine going further in the improvement of research and practice in chapter 12.

Finding out more

Alasuutari, P. (1998) *An Invitation to Social Research* London: Sage Publications Ltd.

Knight, P.Y. (2002) *Small-Scale Research: Pragmatic Inquiry in Social Science and the Caring Professions* London: Sage Publications (particularly on claims-making in small-scale practitioner research).

LSRC (2002) *Research Strategy 2002-5 Influencing the Future: informing policy and improving practice through research* London: Learning and Skills Development Agency

May, T. (1999) *Social Research: Issues, Methods and Process* (2nd edition reprint) Buckingham: Open University Press.

Wilkinson, D. (2000) *The Researcher's Toolkit: The Complete Guide to Practitioner Research* London: RoutledgeFalmer.

Wisker, G.W. *The Postgraduate Research Handbook: Succeed with your MA, MPHil, EdD and PhD* Basingstoke: Plagrave study guides (particularly useful for practitioners studying at postgraduate level who want to make use of their research).

Yin, R.K. (1994) *Case Study Research: Design and Methods* (second edition) London: Sage Publications (particularly useful for practitioners using case study as a small-scale research strategy).

Chapter 12
Going further: joining a community of research practice

Professional development

As we noted in chapter 3, professional knowledge is by its nature incomplete and always changing. Your own knowledge of research will develop as you gain experience in conducting research and reading about the research of others. This book can only begin to address the depth of knowledge and skill that can be acquired in research methodology. As you begin to develop, you will move through the stages outlined by Dreyfus and Dreyfus (1986), where you cease to be a novice and begin to be competent. Like many skills, such competence needs to be kept current. This chapter will help you consider a number of ways to develop your own professional knowledge as a practice-based researcher.

Throughout our book, we have provided examples for people in the further education sector to undertake research into professional practice. Getting started on research need not be a lonely trail to blaze in your institution. The following section provides information about existing routes to gain knowledge and skills in research, about networks that you might like to join, and how you can gain qualifications in research.

The Learning and Skills Research Network

In chapter 1, Andrew Morris, introduced the way in which the LSDA, while it was FEDA, helped to establish and support the

Learning and Skills Research Network (LSRN). There are nine regions in this network, all of which have a regional director at LSDA who supports the work of the regional LSRNs. You can contact them through the LSDA website, and click on 'research' (see http://www.lsda.org.uk). These networks bring together LSC practitioners with researchers from HE who have a particular interest and background in the LSC sector. People attending regional LSRN meetings also come from a range of roles within the FE sector. This creates synergy between FE practitioners as well as between practitioners and researchers. ·

Each regional network has its own way of arranging meetings and events. In the past three years, there have been conferences in many of the regions. These provide a good opportunity for people who have been undertaking research in their institutions to share findings, and hear about the work of colleagues. The regional conferences can provide a starting point for dissemination of research work for many college staff who may be diffident about presenting their research findings to a national audience. The regional aspect of the conferences also allows colleagues to make full use of the geographical contexts in which they work.

Regional networks have been given funds by LSDA to work on small-scale projects. The London and South East Region has undertaken research into the effectiveness of initial teacher training. The North West has examined areas of basic skills in which learners ask for help. These projects have been reported in the publication *Learning and Skills Research Journal*, and can be found on the regional websites.

You do not have to have a research role in your institution to be part of the network. Simply having an interest in this area is enough. Some people do have a specific named responsibility for research in their college, or for supporting the professional development of staff, including initial teacher training. Some members may be undertaking their own postgraduate qualifications, involving a research project. Others are simply keen to participate in opportunities for conducting research, and in finding out about research findings from colleagues in the field.

The toolkit

As Andrew Morris indicated in chapter 1, the LSDA has created a research toolkit which can be used by colleges to help foster research capability amongst staff. At the time of writing, this toolkit is offered free to colleges. A facilitator will work with a group of staff on any chosen topic, and each topic comprises a session of approximately two and a half hours. The topics currently available are

Topic Title

1. Distinguishing research from development

2. Specifying projects

3. Making sense of statistics

4. Designing and using questionnaires

5. Planning and scheduling projects

6. Evaluation

7. Analysis and interpretation of qualitative data

8. Selecting the right research methods

9. Reviewing the literature

10. Working with people in research – ethical issues

11. Interpreting and presenting quantitative data

12. Interviewing people – face to face and by telephone

13. Facilitating focus groups

14. Conveying the message – making reports interesting

15. Writing a research bid/tender

Managers in an LSC institution could decide to introduce a staff development programme drawing upon a number of the toolkit sessions. An individual manager could identify that a research project using a particular research tool might make use of the appropriate toolkit session to ensure the deployment of the tool is effective and operates within necessary ethical and theoretical guidelines.

Other networks

There are numerous online networks that you can join. *Mailbase* is particularly useful. Although not strictly research based, much of the discussion and dissemination of ideas stems from research issues. For the Learning and Skills Sector, there are a number of groups to which you may wish to subscribe including

*   Association of Colleges (AoC)

*   Information and Learning Technology (ILT)

NIACE is particularly helpful with facilitating networks. For email discussion groups for learning and skills listed by NIACE see

*   http://www.niace.org.uk/information/Forms/ListSubscribe.asp

NIACE also provides a briefing sheet in .pdf format on using mail-groups – available at: http://www.niace.org.uk/information/Briefing _sheets/Mailgroups.pdf

There are a number of groups including

*   ACLF Email Group (support and information relating to the Adult & Community Learning Fund (ACLF)

*   Basic Skills (issues and information relating to Basic Skills)

*   Lifelong Learning (issues relating to Lifelong Learning)

*   Making IT Accessible (support group for the IT community lap-top project)

*   Older Learners (support group for older learners)

*   Black Practitioners and Learners Network(formerly called the Racially Inclusive Learning Network – issues relating to minority ethnic learners and practitioners)

*   Women Learning (issues particularly relating to women learn-ing)

There are also particular networks facilitated by LSDA (http://www. lsda.org.uk) including:

*   Staff Development Network (LSDA and NASDN)

*   Marketing

As noted in chapter 11, there are resources on research methodology, and a significant number of journals publishing research articles relating to FE practice. You can check which journals are most appropriate by browsing through your library, and many of the journals have contents pages online. The LSC has an electronic newsletter to which you can subscribe . It is called the Skills and Education Network, 'skillsandedu' and can be found on http://www. lsc@abcon.net. This provides news in brief, reviews, a monthly feature, an events diary and 'coming soon' section. There are good links to other government and agency websites.

Conferences

Although these can be expensive to attend, particularly if they are residential, conferences are a wonderful source of research networking. You will meet people who share your interest. They may have their own research projects which you might want to follow through and even replicate in your own institution. Conferences also enable you to 'cascade' the information that you gain from your attendance, and word of mouth is still one of the most potent ways of hearing about new ideas and sharing information.

Participating at conferences

If you want to give a paper at a conference, then here are some pointers to ensure that you are successful.

Always read the conference publicity and calls for papers carefully. Does the conference theme apply to your research? Could your research be 'loosely' connected to the theme, even if it is not directly applicable? Are the conference delegates likely to be interested in your area of research?

If you are asked to provide an abstract, make sure that you keep to the word limit. Remember that the abstract tells the conference planning team what to expect from your presentation. You do not need to provide the full research project in an abstract! Think of it as a 'sound bite', in which you tell people the subject of your paper, something about the way in which you conducted the research, and some preliminary findings. If you have not yet finished your research, do not let that stop you putting in a proposal. There is nothing like a deadline to write a paper to present at a conference to ensure that it gets written! If your paper is accepted, the abstract will also inform the delegates about your research, as the abstracts are usually printed in the conference programme to help delegates decide which sessions to attend.

There are different types of presentation at conferences. The most traditional is *'giving a paper'*. This means that you have a short length of time to present the main points of your paper and then have time for the delegates to raise questions. Often, more than one paper is presented in a session. If the conference planners are well organised, they may try to place papers with common themes in one session. However, some conferences do not have themes, and the papers are then quite disparate.

Workshops are meant to be more participative than lecture style sessions. Here, instead of making a presentation, the presenter engages the delegates in activities. For example, you may have undertaken research into a different style of learning activity, and you want the delegates to experience this at first hand so that they can provide comments and discuss the implications of using the activity in their own situations. Unfortunately, many people make the mistake of giving a paper at a workshop session, and the delegates remain passive. If you are going to offer to run a workshop, make sure that you have a clear idea of what it is you are going to do, including what you want the delegates to do.

Round table discussions are another way in which you can take part in a conference.In a round table discussion, you decide on a topic which you wish to discuss with conference delegates. You may have a number of issues arising from aspects of your research that you wish to test out with your peers, or you may want to use the results of a round table discussion to inform the way in which you develop your research project. Again, as with workshops, it is important not to take the time up by making a presentation. With round table discussions, try to create a number of questions that delegates can respond to, or at least have an idea of how you wish to facilitate discussion if you wish to negotiate the content when the delegates arrive.

If you have never given a paper and are very nervous about doing so, *poster presentations* are a good way to get started. Instead of reading out some of your ideas to an assembled group of delegates in a session, or making a presentation from slides, you place your ideas visually on a poster, and delegates come and look at them. They may be on view throughout the conference or there may be a set time for the poster presentations. In the case of the latter, you would stand by your poster and talk to people as they wander along and look. You would provide details of how you can be contacted, so that interested delegates could follow up queries.

A conference paper may be required to be in a particular house style by the conference organisers. There may be a date by which you must submit the paper before you are guaranteed a place at the conference. This means that you must plan your time carefully. At other conferences, you may be asked to bring copies of your paper to distribute to interested delegates. We prefer the system in which you ask people who want a copy of your paper to provide you with an email address, or their full address so that you can send them a copy. This does, at least, help preserve the consumption of paper. You can never tell how many people will attend your session, and if you are asked to bring multiple copies of your paper, these are often wasted.

Writing a conference paper should follow the guidelines for writing research reports in chapter 11.

Qualifications in research

Most postgraduate degrees contain a requirement to undertake a piece of investigation into a topic of your choice. With MSc degrees in particular, there is usually a taught research methods component which is a requirement for those proceeding to the research project and dissertation phase of their studies. There are as many different programmes on research methods as there are postgraduate degrees. Some require attendance at a number of taught sessions which lead to the development of a research proposal which includes a literature search.

Some degree programmes may place a heavy influence on qualitative research, others on quantitative research. If you are considering studying for a postgraduate degree, do make sure that you consult the prospectus and identify what kind of research methods programmes are on offer.

There are usually set timescales for gaining a postgraduate degree. Some part time courses have an attendance requirement over two years, followed by three months to undertake a research project and write the dissertation. Others are more flexible, possibly with a modular structure, which enables you to dip in and out of the programme according to your own commitments at work and at home. It is important that you find out what the programme offers and requires in terms of flexibility. If you know that you are very busy during the time that assessment of work takes place on one of the programmes, it is clearly not a sensible one to consider.

There are postgraduate degrees available by distance learning. The Open University pioneered this approach, and its research methods programme, particularly in post-compulsory education, is very thorough. However, the programme has changed recently and now contains an element of research in each of the modules offered. You can take any module as a stand alone course, which leads to a certificate in that subject area.

A more demanding research degree is the doctorate programme, the PhD or the professional doctorate in education, the EdD. In this, you are expected to have a postgraduate qualification or equivalent experience, and you work on an individual basis with a supervisor, investigating a particular research topic that you have identified in a preliminary preparatory phase. This research degree is only suitable for people who are very committed to undertaking research and can work autonomously with a minimum of supervision. If you do register for a doctorate, you will normally be required to undertake a programme of research methods, unless you have a Masters degree which demonstrates that you have covered this in sufficient detail. The criteria for gaining a PhD is that you have made a significant contribution to knowledge. This is not easy to do.

The EdD is different from a PhD in that it has more taught components, and usually requires an investigation into an aspect of professional practice. Many people, including research supervisors, struggle to distinguish between differing characteristics of a Phd and an EdD. It is more than the fact that the latter has a larger teaching component. The EdD is also meant to reflect an examination of professional practice, whereas a PhD is an examination of any phenomenon or topic.

If you are not sure which is the best programme of study to pursue, then do make an appointment to visit a research tutor at your local higher education institution. If you have more than one institution, go and visit several. With doctoral level study, you will spend a lot of time with your supervisor, and it is important to ensure that you are going to have a productive relationship. You do not need to be friends with your supervisor, but you do need to have confidence in this person, and be clear about how you will work together (Phillips and Pugh, 2000)

Finding time to undertake a programme of study for a research qualification is without doubt very demanding. You must read the literature on your topic thoroughly, and keep up to date as you progress through your own research. You will need to spend time choosing and piloting your methodology. You must find ways to gain access to the people and organisations on which you intend to focus your research. You need a great deal of time to organise and conduct the fieldwork. You need time to analyse your data and think about the implications of your findings. And of course, you need time to write your thesis, which for a traditional PhD is usually around 80,000 words.

If this sounds daunting, the satisfaction that is derived from achieving such an award is truly amazing. You will have shown that you can manage a project through to the end and that you can juggle your time with the host of commitments that you already have in your busy life. And of course, you will have contributed to knowledge about the sector, and provide important information for others who will follow after. It is by undertaking research degrees that individuals within the sector can raise the capacity for research.

Facilitating research practices in your own organisation

As there is increasing higher education provision within the further education sector in particular, staff must show that they are research active. If you are a manager in your organisation, it is likely that you will need to consider how you can support the research activity and meet funding council requirements.

You may decide that a way forward to ensure that practitioners in your institution and in your field are research active is to start working towards organisational and structural means to create a research culture. This is a long term strategy, but one which will pay great dividends if successful. There are examples of colleges which have already used this process. In the 1990s, Suffolk College took a proactive approach to foster research capability. The college created a post of director of research and it provided funds for staff development (this was in the time of the FEFC funding and before the Standards Fund had been created). There was a staff conference to share and disseminate research findings, and the college produced a series of research publications in house, which were also distributed in the further education sector.

Another institution in the South East, Northbrook College, is a college which specialises in art and design. Most people do not associate this subject area with research. Yet the principal of the college fostered a research approach by using funding to enhance research capability through conference attendance, and through a publication, which like the Suffolk College publications, was circulated both within the college and outside. In this publication, there would generally be a reflective analysis of some aspect of teaching and learning, along with examples of research undertaken by staff in the college.

Another way to keep research on the agenda in your institution is to include it as an agenda item in meetings. There are planning meetings in every institution, which require data and evidence to make decisions for future activities. Taking a more critical and analytical stance towards the figures provided, and creating questions that test the assumptions made, is a good way to ensure that research maintains a higher profile.

As individuals, you can circulate information gained from research journals and articles to your colleagues. If you are fortunate enough to have a staff common room, you can create a pack of information that is passed on from one colleague to another. You may begin to store research findings in your office, so that colleagues can consult them as issues arise.

Although it may seem as though you are involved in extra work, once you develop a habit of keeping newspaper cuttings, references to appropriate articles and books in a consistent way, it soon leads to a wonderful resource for yourself and your colleagues. It is even better if your colleagues also add to your resource base, providing that you devise a way to keep track of what is being deposited.

You can also share information and resources electronically. If your institution supports a virtual learning environment (VLE), you could create a space for research interests. Colleagues could upload papers and information they have obtained electronically, or list links to websites, and of course, have online discussions about particular topics. As with all online discussions, these are best organised through facilitators and by agreeing parameters.

Keep on reading

Finally, if you are interested in research, but are unable to undertake any yourself, this does not mean that you are research 'inactive'. One of the most important ways to keep up to date is to read about other research which is reported. We have already discussed the variety of sources for research literature in chapter 6. Here, we simply want to remind you that anything that you read may prove to be worthwhile later on. You may remember a snippet from a newspaper article that will launch you into a new way of thinking, or practice. As long as you reflect on what you have read, and analysed the implications of what has been said, you will be engaging in the kind of activity which is monitoring situations, almost as if you are using antenna to sense the world around you. This is a crucial aspect of any research endeavour and should not be underestimated.

Conclusion

We hope you have enjoyed reading about research and how you can undertake it in the further education and the wider Learning and Skills sector. We understand the demands of professional practice in the sector. We also understand how hard it is to find time to undertake research if it is not part of your role. We hope you will feel inspired to 'have a go' at small-scale research, and that you will make connections with colleagues from your institution and further afield who share your interest in research.

At a time when the government is relying heavily on the Learning and Skills Sector to deliver many of its aims in fostering lifelong learning for all, it is vital that the professionals in the sector have the capacity to undertake research.

Practitioners need to be enabled to provide good evidence-based research to inform policy-making, based on authentic daily FE practice carried out with learners. Policies more explicitly linked to practice will facilitate improved access to learning opportunities, which will be of greater benefit to people, their families and the people they live and work with. We have therefore written this book for practitioners in the FE sector and for the benefit of learners who are at the heart of all of our work.

Finding out more

LSRC (2002) *Research Strategy 2002-5 Influencing the Future: informing policy and improving practice through research* London: Learning and Skills Development Agency

References

Adonis, A. (1996, 15th December) Let Blair be his own education chief *Observer* article: archive available at: http://www.observer.co.uk/education/story/0,12554,820319,00. html

Alasuutari, P. (1998) An Invitation to Social Research London: Sage Publications

Attwell, G., Jennes, A., and Tomassini, M. (1997), Work-related Knowledge and Work Process Knowledge in A.Brown (ed) *Promoting vocational education and training: European perspectives* Tampere: University of Tampere Press

Bell, J. (1993) *Doing your Research Project* (2nd edn) Buckingham: Open University Press

Bell, J., and Opie, C. (2002) *Learning from Research: Getting more from your data* Buckingham: Open University Press

British Educational Research Association BERA (1992) *Ethical Guidelines for Educational Research* BERA downloadable on http://www.bera.ac.uk

Blaxter, L., Hughes, C., and Tight, M. (1996) *How to Research* Buckingham: Open University Press

Bloomer, M. (1997) *Curriculum making in Post-16 Education: the social Conditions of Studentship* London: Routledge

Brookfield, S.D. (1995) *Becoming a Critically Reflective Teacher* San Francisco: Jossey Bass

Bryman, A. and Cramer, D. (1990) *Quantitative Data Analysis for Social Scientists* London: Routledge

Chalmers, A.F. (1982) *What is this thing called Science?* Buckingham: Open University Press

Chisholm, M. (2001) *The Internet Guide for Writers* Oxford: How to Books Ltd.

Cohen, L., Manion, L., and Morrison, K. (2000) *Research methods in education* (5th edn) London: Routledge

Covey, S. (1999) *The Seven Habits of Highly Effective People* (reissued edition) London: Simon & Schuster

Cowan, J. (1999) *On Becoming an Innovative University Teacher* Buckingham: Open University Press

Davies P. (2001) *Closing the achievement gap: colleges making a difference*, LSDA

Denscome, M. (2002) *Ground Rules for Good Research: a 10 point guide for social researchers* Buckingham: Open University Press

Department for Education and Employment (1998) *The Learning Age: A Renaissance for New Britain* London: The Stationery Office

Department for Education and Employment (1999) *Learning to Succeed* London: The Stationery Office

Department for Education and Skills (2002a) *Success for All* London: The Stationery Office

Department for Education and Skills (2002b) *Educational and Skills: Delivering Results, A Strategy to 2006* Suffolk: DfES Publications

Desforges, C. (2001) Keynote address at the Learning and Skills Research Network Annual Conference, Robinson College, Cambridge, December 2001

De Vaus, D. (2002) *Analyzing Social Science Data: 50 Key Problems in Data Analysis* London: Sage

Dewey, J. (1933) *How we think: A Restatement of the Relation of Reflective Thinking in the Educative Process* Chicago: Henry Regnery

Dreyfus, H., and Dreyfus, S. (1986) *Mind over Machine: The Power of Intuition and Expertise in the Era of the Computer* Oxford: Blackwell

Dunford, J. (2002) NFER Council Address by Dr John Dunford, General Secretary, Secondary Heads Association, 15th October 2002, *Research Evidence and Government Policy – the need for a stronger connection.* On-line paper available at NFER website: http://www.nfer.ac.uk/research/papers/Council02.doc

Elliot, J. (1991) 'A Model of Professionalism and its Implication for Teacher Education' *British Educational Research Journal* 17 (4) 310-14

Eraut M. (1994) *Developing Professional Knowledge and Competence* London: Falmer

Eraut, M., Alderton, J., and Cole, G. (1998) *Development of knowledge and skills in employment* Research report no 5 University of Sussex: University of Sussex, Institute of Education

Further Education Funding Council (1997) *Learning works Report of the Committee on Widening Participation in Further Education*, chaired by Baroness Kennedy. Coventry: FEFC

Further Education National Training Organisation (FENTO) (2001) *National Occupational Standards for Management in Further Education* London: FENTO

Further Education National Training Organisation (FENTO) (1999) *Standards for Teaching and Supporting Learning in Further Education in England and Wales* London: FENTO

Flanagan, J.C. (1954) The Critical Incident Technique *Psychological Bulletin* 51 (4) 327-58

Gawel, J.E. (1997). *Herzberg's Theory of Motivation and Maslow's Hierarchy of Needs.* ERIC/AE Digest article, ERIC Clearinghouse on Assessment and Evaluation Washington DC.

Giddens, A. (1984) *The Constitution of Society*, Polity Press, Oxford

Gillham, B. (2000) *The research interview* London: Continuum

Glaser B.G., and Strauss A.L. (1967) *The Discovery of Grounded Theory: Strategies for Qualitative Research* London: Weidenfeld and Nicolson

Gough, C. (2000) *Completing the Research Project*, in David Wilkinson (ed.) The Researchers' Toolkit, London: RoutledgeFalmer

Habermas, J. (1974) *Theory and Practice* London: Heinemann

Habermas, J., (1987) *Knowledge and Human Interests*, English translation Cambridge: Polity Press

Hammersley, M. (2003) Can and Should Educational Research be Educative? *Oxford Review of Education* 29 (1) pp3-25

Harkin, J., Clow, R., and Hillier, Y., (2003) *Reflected in Tranquility? FE teachers' perceptions of their initial teacher training* London: Learning and Skills Development Agency

Hart, C. (2001) *Doing a Literature Search* Buckingham: Open University Press

Hillier, Y. (2002) *Reflective Teaching in Further and Adult Education* London: Continuum

Hodge, M. (2002) Keynote address at the Learning and Skills Research Network Annual Conference, University of Warwick, 12th December 2002

Hodgson, A. (2000) *Policies, Politics and the Future of Lifelong Learning*, Series: The Future of Education from 14+ London: Kogan Page

Hodgson, A., and Spours, K. (1999) *New Labour's Educational Agenda: Issues and Policies for Education and Training*, Series: The Future of Education from 14+ London: Kogan Page

Jameson, J., and Hillier, Y. (2003) *Researching Post-Compulsory Education* London: Continuum

Johnson, M. (1997) *Research in FE Colleges* Research Report No 1. London: Further Education Development Agency

Kennedy, H. (1997) *Learning Works: Widening Participation in Further Education* Coventry: FEFC

Knight, P.Y. (2002) *Small-Scale Research: Pragmatic Inquiry in Social Science and the Caring Professions* London: Sage Publications.

Kuhn, T. (1970) *The structure of scientific revolutions* Chicago: University of Chicago Press

Lave, E., and Wenger, E. (1991) *Situated learning* Cambridge: Cambridge University Press

Learning and Skills Council (2002) *Seeking Views of Learners: Findings from the LSC's first national learner satisfaction survey 2001/02 Summary Report* Coventry: Learning and Skills Council

Learning and Skills Research Centre (2002) *Research Strategy 2002-5 Influencing the Future: informing policy and improving practice through research* London: Learning and Skills Development Agency

Lewin, K. (1948) *Resolving Social Conflicts* New York: Harper

Maslow, A. H. (1970) *Motivation and Personality* (2nd ed.). New York: Harper and Row (on Malslow's hierarchy of needs)

May, T. (1999) *Social Research: Issues, Methods and Process* (2nd edition reprint) Buckingham: Open University Press.

McNiff, J., Lomax, P., and Whitehead, J. (1996) *You and your Action Research Project* London: Routledge

Milgram, S. (1963) Behavior Study of Obedience, *Journal of Abnormal and Social Psychology* 67, 371-8.

Milgram, S. (1964) Group Pressure and Action against a Person, *Journal of Abnormal and Social Psychology* 69, 137-43.

Morris, A. (2002) *From Idea to Impact: A guide to the research process*, London: Learning and Skills Research Centre

Organisation for Economic Co-operation and Development (2002) *Educational Research and Development in England: Examiners Report,* Paris: OECD Centre for Educational Research and Innovation

Orna, E. and Stevens, J. (1995) *Managing Information for Research* Buckingham: Open University Press

Peters J.M. (1994) Instructors as Researchers-and-theorists: Faculty Development in a Community College in R.Benn and R.Fieldhouse (eds) *Training and Development in Adult and Continuing Education* Exeter: CRCE

Phillips, E.M., and Pugh, D.S. (2000) *How to get a PhD: a handbook for students and their supervisors* Buckingham: Open University Press

Popper, K. (1972) *The Logic of Scientific Discovery* London: Hutchinson

Robson, C. (1993) *Real World Research: A Resource for Social Scientists and Practitioner-Researchers* Oxford: Blackwell Publishers Ltd.

Ryan, A.B. (2001) *Feminist ways of knowing: towards theorising the person for radical adult education* Leicester: NIACE (questions of human subjectivity, discourse and feminism)

Ryle, G. (1949) *The concept of mind* London: Hutchinson

Saunders, M. (1985) *Emerging Issues for TVEI Implementation* (2nd edn). Lancaster: University of Lancaster

Scholfield, P. (1995) *Quantifying Language: A Researcher's and Teacher's Guide to Gathering Language Data and Reducing it to Figures* Clevedon: Multilingual Matters Ltd.

Schön, D. (1983) *The Reflective Practitioner* New York: Basic Books

Schön, D. (1987) *Educating the Reflective Practitioner: Towards a New Design for Teaching and Learning in the Professions* San Francisco: Jossey Bass

Scott, D. (2000) *Reading Educational Research and Policy* RoutledgeFalmer: London

Simons, H. (1980) *Towards a Science of the Singular* Norwich: Centre for Applied Research in Education, University of Anglia

Stenhouse, L. (1975) *An Introduction to Curriculum Research and Development* London: Heinemann

Strauss, A., and Corbin, J.M.(1990) *Basic of Qualitative research: grounded theory procedures and techniques* London: Sage

Taylor, S. (2002) *Attracting new learners: international evidence and practice,* London: LSDA

Wilkinson, D. (2000) *The Researcher's Toolkit: The Complete Guide to Practitioner Research* London: RoutledgeFalmer.

Wisker, G.W. (2001) *The Postgraduate Research Handbook: Succeed with your MA, MPHil, EdD and PhD* Basingstoke: Plagrave study guides.

Yin, R.K. (1994) *Case Study Research: Design and Methods* (second edition) London: Sage Publications

Index

A levels 28
accuracy 61, 154
action research xx, xxii, 51, 53, 55
   emancipatory xx, 55
   practical xx
   technical xx,
action research group 92, 167
Adult Learning Inspectorate (ALI) 143
applied research 10
appropriate measures 144
AS levels 28
authenticity 61, 168
authorship 92
average 147-149
   arithmetic mean 148, 149
   median 148, 149
   mode 147, 149
bar chart 147
baseline information 60
benchmarks 143, 144
bias 87, 120, 132, 135, 152, 153
   accurate reflection 93, 120
   conflicting stories 96
   cultural 149
   misrepresentation 93
   skewing interpretation 117, 151
bibliography 74, 81, 82
BIDS Bath Information Database Service 78
brainstorming 75
briefing and debriefing 86, 89

case study *see* research methods
categories 43, 116
   goodness of fit 118
CEDEFOP 4
Chi Square 158-159
closed questions *see* questions
coding *see also* data analysis 135, 139
coding responses 117
collaboration xviii, 6, 7, 11, 13, 17, 55, 168
collaborative approach 6
communicate findings *see also* dissemination 5, 167
community 14, 51, 97
community of practice xviii, xx, xxii
practice based knowledge
conferences 9, 13, 167, 179-181
   abstract 179
   call for papers 179
   giving a paper 180
   poster presentation 180
   round table 180
   workshop 180
consent 87, 95
consent form 87, 88
constraints 44, 64
CPD continuing professional development xix, 167
control groups 85, 95
correlation 155, 157
cost benefit analysis 92

COVE Centre for Vocational Excellence 22
critical evaluation 32
critical incidents 52
critical lenses 52
cross tabulation 158
culture of change 15
culture of research 14, 184
data
   continuous 145, 155
   definition 153
   discrete 145
   interval 153, 154
   nominal 153, 158
   ordinal 145, 153, 154
   qualitative 154
   quantitative 154
   rank order 145, 147
   raw data 117
data analysis 11, 12, 47, 61, 62, 115, 124, 146
   permission to quote 120
   software 118
   Atlas-Ti 118
   Nu-dist 118
data collection 11, 12
data interpretation 12
   weasel words 119
Data Protection Act 66, 90
data recording 61
databases 143
degrees of freedom 159
DfES xxi, 23
   Strategic framework 19

dissemination *see also*
    presentation of
    findings 66, 171-174,
    176, 184, 185
economic issues 23
educational improvement 20
educational policy 21, 25-
    28
empiricists 37
employer training pilots 22
empowerment xx, xxi, 33,
    51
EPPI – Centre for
    Evidence-informed
    Education xxi, 28
Policy and Practice
    Information
equal opportunities 24
ES – Employment Service
    18
ESRC Economic and Social
    Research Council 8
ethics 39, 62, 66
    anonymity 66, 85, 86,
    89, 125, 134
    confidentiality 68, 85,
    89, 105, 111, 115, 134
    definition 83
    principles 83
    protection 83
    code of ethics 84, 177
        BERA 85, 96
        DfES 85, 96
        NFER 85
        QCA 85, 96
evaluation
    evaluation of change
    56
    findings 62
    iterative process 57
    monitoring of change
    56
evidence based research
    xxi, 4, 13, 25, 27, 28,
    32, 48
excellence 16
experiments 38
fairness 134
FEDA Further Education
    Development Agency
    xxi, 4
FEFC Further Education
    Funding Council 17

FENTO Further Education
    National Training
    Organisation xix, 125
FERN Further Education
    Research Network
    xxi, 5
FEU Further Education
    Unit 4
FHE Act Further and
    Higher Education Act
    17
focus groups *see also*
    interviews 112-113,
    130
framing questions of
    research 35, 46, 61,
    68, 71, 77
frequencies *see also* data,
    statistics 147, 148
    fractions, decimals
    and percentages 146
funding body 64, 67
    requirements 64
funding initiatives 21
    commissioned
    research 54
    bidding for funds 169
fuzzy ideas 44
GNVQ General Vocational
    Qualifications 27, 28
governance 24
Grounded Theory 43, 44,
    117
Harvard referencing system
    81
HEFCE Higher Education
    Funding Council for
    England 8
HND Higher National
    Diploma 27, 28
hypothesis 38, 39, 55, 60,
    94, 157
    testing hypotheses 44,
    55, 60
impact of research 10, 11,
    13
information analysis 72
    authority 72
    brainstorm 74, 75
    metaphors 75
    relevance 72
information management
    118

information retrieval 74
    google 78, 80
    meta-search engine 79
    ranking algorithm 78
information sources 59, 65,
    72, 73
    audio-visual 73
    citation index 79
        AHCI Arts and
        Humanities 81
        SSCI Social
        Science Citation
        Index 81
    citing sources 72
    date of sources 77
    gaps 76
    web based 73, 74, 78,
    79
information strategy 72, 74
    selectivity 72, 76, 81
    keyword search 78, 81
ILT – information learning
    technology 18, 24,
    165
informed consent 85, 86,
    134
    right to withdraw 134
initiatives – funding 21
innovation fatigue 21
interviews 47, 99-121
    advantages 100, 101,
    102, 121
    disadvantages 100,
    101, 102, 121
    group 111, 116
    focus group 112, 113,
    130
    follow up interviews
    125, 132
    semi structured 101,
    102, 106
    structured 100, 101
    telephone 110
    unstructured 102
    web based 111
interview organisation 106,
    107, 108
interview recording – *see
    also* data recording
    108, 116
    note taking 108, 109,
    110
    permission to record
    108, 109, 110

video recording 110, 116
keeping up to date 166
knowledge construction 38, 60
knowledge, forms of 8, 36, 37
  codified 36
  explicit 36
  personal 36
  practice based xxi, 11
  process 36
  propositional 36
  tacit 36, 75
knowledge – scientific approach 38
knowledge and theory 10
knowledge transfer 7
knowledge transformation 9, 11
large scale research 54
LEA Local Education Authority 4
Learning and Skills Research Journal 9, 12, 176
Learning to Succeed 20
lifelong learning 19
  14-16, 21, 54
  16-19, 21
  post-16 learning 22
lifelong learning policy 19
Likert scale *see also* questionnaires 137
literature review *see also* information strategy 65, 71-82
LLSC Local Learning and Skills Council 4
LSC Learning and Skills Council xvii, 17, 169
  educational provision 22
LSDA Learning and Skills Development Agency xxi, 7, 8, 54, 169
LSRC Learning and Skills Research Centre 10, 28
LSRN Learning and Skills Research Network 8, 12, 28, 176
making a difference 54

market research 6, 112, 165
MIS management information system 28
ND National Diploma 27, 28
network – practitioner 5, 12, 168, 178
  critical friend 167, 168
  FE research fellowship 169
  mentor 168
  supervisor 168, 183
network – regional research 8, 9, 178
neutrality 26
New Deal 28, 46
NFER National Foundation for Educational Research 10, 28, 85
normal distribution 148-9
  bell curve 148
  Gaussian curve 148
note taking *see* data analysis
null hypothesis 160
OECD Organisation for Economic Co-operation and Development 10
ownership of data *see also* data analysis 91
paradigm 39, 40
  illuminative 40, 42
  incommensurate 40
  scientific 40, 42, 94
  shift 40
physical laws 38
pie chart 146, 147
pilot 105, 112, 131, 133
policy
  policy change 15, 18, 22
  policy documents 23, 25, 26, 27
  policy implementation 26
  policy legislation 23
  policy models 27
  policy long term planning 22
  top down policies 23, 24

power 32, 91, 106, 109
  relationship between researcher and researched 90, 106, 109
practitioner research 11, 53
presentation of findings *see also* dissemination 59, 61, 62, 170-174
  guidelines for writing research reports 171-174181
privacy 85, 86, 89
proactive 32
professional development 6, 13
professional knowledge 35-37, 52, 175
  competence 36, 175
professionalism 93
project design 13, 62-70
project goals 59, 60
project management 6
project planning 59-71
  access 62, 66, 67, 77, 114
  aims and objectives 65, 123, 135
  audience 136
  context 62, 64, 68
  decision matrix 62, 63
  goals 59, 60
  permission 67, 114
  proposal 63, 64
  research brief 45
  resources 59, 64, 65, 124
  strategy 130
  strengths and weaknesses 71
  timescale 62-65, 67, 124
pseudonym 89
publication of research *see also* dissemination 7, 9
qualifications in research xix, 12, 67, 97, 166, 176, 181, 182
quality performance 24
powerstories 26, 27
questionnaires xxii, 41, 123
  advantages 124
  disadvantages 131

response rates 132
security precautions 133
questionnaire analysis *see also* data analysis 124
accuracy 130, 131, 135
automatic reader scanner 130, 139
coding 137
distortion 131
Likert Scale 137
self-completed questionnaire 124, 125, 126, 130, 137
questions 103
closed questions 105, 137
open questions 42, 105, 137
prompts 101
QUILT Quality in Information Learning and Teaching 9
R and D Toolkit xxii, 6, 177
RAE Research Assessment Exercise 8
RDA Regional Development Agency 4
Reflection 6, 16, 55
reflective analysis 32
reflective awareness 25
meta-cognitive awareness 25, 26
reflexivity 25
reflective practice xxii , 51-57
reflection in action 52
reflection on action 52
regional workshops 29
regionality 8
relationship between researcher and researched 84
relationship between variables 147
relativism 94
reliability 44
research approaches 41, 61, 69
research – definition xvii, xviii
research capacity 185

research methods xxii, 65
advantages and disadvantages 69
case study 70, 130
desk based 69
qualitative 41
quantitative 41
observation 130
online 130
research outcomes 47, 61, 65
research rationale 56, 61, 123
research tools 41, 56
RQA Raising Achievement and Quality 9
Sampling 150-153
oversampling 152
random 152
representation 150
sample size 153
strategy 150
stratified 152
systematic 152
scope 61, 77
sectoral knowledge 15
sensitivity 134, 174
significance 158, 160
small scale research 48, 166, 176, 185
software *see* data analysis
SPSS Statistical Package for Social Sciences 130
staff issues 24, 165
stages of research planning *see also* project management 7
standard deviation 150
statistical error 155
type 1 error 160
type 2 error 160
statistical measures – accuracy 144
statistical tests 154, 155
non-parametric 155
parametric 155
power of 161
statistics – use of xxii, 143-161
strategies for research impact 10
post-16 education and training 11

practitioner research findings 170-172
Success for All 16
systematic enquiry 55
teacher based research 3
technical issues of research 6
TECs Training and Enterprise Councils 3, 18
themes 43, 116, 119
spidergram, exploded thematic chart 42
theoretical models 60
fields of study 61, 69
institutional 60
psychological 60
sociological 60
transcripts *see also* data analysis 105, 115, 117
trends 24, 146, 151
trial and error 55
truth 85, 93
TVEI Training and Vocational Education Initiative 3, 29
typology of institutional responses 29-32
accommodating 31
over-compliant 31
reflexive 32
resistant 30
universal laws 40
usefulness of research 8, 10, 165
validity 41, 61, 135
value laden 27
variables 38, 39, 153, 154
dependent 157
independent 157
Venn diagram 45, 157
what works *see also* usefulness of research 35, 53
widening participation 166
workshops 9, 180